PRIME TIME TOGETHER...
With Kids

Creative Ideas, Activities, Games, and Projects

Donna Erickson

Illustrated by David LaRochelle

This edition published and distributed exclusively
by Discovery Toys, Inc.

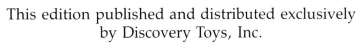

To my parents, John and Joan Anduri,
who baked cookies, built the best swing sets in the world,
heard my bedtime prayers, and by their example
taught me the importance of a loving and supportive family.

PRIME TIME TOGETHER . . . WITH KIDS
Creative Ideas, Activities, Games, and Projects

First published in 1989 by Augsburg Fortress.
Copyright © 1989 Augsburg Fortress

The "Gadget Band" activity on pp. 104-105 is based on Minneapolis composer/ performer Monica Maye's "Home Appliance Orchestra," copyright © 1988, as presented at Walker Art Center, Minneapolis, Minnesota, and Southeastern Center for Contemporary Arts, Winston-Salem, North Carolina. Used by permission.

The "Alphabet Art" activity on pp. 110-111 is used with permission of Jane Lundquist.

Library of Congress Cataloging-in-Publication Data

Erickson, Donna, 1949–
    Prime time together . . . with kids: creative ideas, activities, games, and projects / Donna Erickson : illustrations by David LaRochelle.
        p.   cm.
    Includes index.
    ISBN 0-8066-2430-2
    1. Creative activities and art work.   1. Title.
    GV1203.E675   1989
    649'.51—dc20   89-6956
                                                                      CIP

METRIC CONVERSION CHART
The following conversion table will assist readers more familiar with metric measurements in following activity instructions throughout this book.

U. S. Standard		Metric Equivalent
Volumetric Measurements		
1 Teaspoon (t, tsp.)	=	4.93 milliliters (ml)
1 Tablespoon (T, Tbs.)	=	14.79 milliliters (ml)
1 Cup (c.)	=	.24 liters (L)
1 Quart (qt.)	=	.95 liters (L)
1 Gallon (gal.)	=	3.8 liters (L)
1 Pound (lb.)	=	453.6 grams (g)
Linear Measurements		
1 inch (in., ")	=	2.53 centimeters (cm)
1 foot (ft., ')	=	.305 meters (m)
1 yard (yd.)	=	.914 meters (m)
1 mile (mi.)	=	1.61 kilometers (km)
Oven Settings		
140°F (Fahrenheit)	=	60°C (Celsius)
350°F (Fahrenheit)	=	177°C (Celsius)

Contents

Introduction

Prime time together—it sounds like television. And actually, this book grew out of ideas I have shared with television viewers. But *Prime Time Together . . . with Kids* is not about TV. It's about kids and adults and having fun.

The activities in this book are designed for adults and children to do *together*. They are meant to help build relationships between adult and child and to foster self-esteem and creativity.

I believe children are a gift for us to nurture and enjoy. To do this well takes time, and that offers a challenge to our culture's obsession with speed. Everything today must be done quickly: instant weight loss, one-hour photo processing, fast food. We are becoming conditioned to value the current trend only until the next one comes along. But the wisdom of old must not be forgotten: "Anything worthwhile takes time." Raising kids takes time. It's hard to imagine a parent saying at a child's graduation, "I wish I hadn't spent so much time with my child." Just as in times past, commitment, discipline, and dedication to our children are required of modern parents if we are to pass on the truths, values, and traditions important to us. Time spent establishing a solid and caring family unit is vital for equipping our children to deal with the changes and challenges they will face throughout their lives.

But parents are busy people. Work related projects take up much of our time. Time spent at the office, time spent working around the house, time spent shopping and running errands, time spent at meetings and socializing, time spent on ourselves—all cut into the time spent with our children. Guilt creeps into the picture when important family time is not part of the regular routine. Today's parents are faced with the dilemma of distinguishing between "quality time" and "quantity time." I prefer not to use those labels. Time spent with children—no matter what amount—is *important* time. And parents need to address that fact. They can continue to feel guilty about the priorities that have shaped their life-styles, or they can take some steps to change their situation. One step is to involve children in their day-to-day activities.

Including children in adult activities is rarely the most efficient way to get things done. Little "helping" hands may actually create *more* work. A friend of mine related this story about her childhood:

Every spring, when it was time for planting, Dad would call me out to the barn to help him get the machinery ready. He always said, "Mary, I need you to do a special job that can only be done with small hands like yours. My hands are too big to turn some of the screws and bolts." And so I would spend several happy days with my dad, helping him prepare for planting. It wasn't until I was about 35 that it occurred to me that Dad never really needed those small hands. Quite frankly, I think I put his schedule behind a week because of my "assistance." But he kept asking for me, year after year.

If, like that father, more parents realized how much they have to offer their children, parenting would be more positive. It's not always the success of the activity we do, or the activity itself, but the time shared with our children that makes the difference. You don't have to be an expert to be a good parent. But, you must be willing to spend time with your child. Doing things together can foster self-confidence in both child and adult.

The environment surrounding children is a primary factor in leading them toward their full, creative potential. Parents, caregivers, and teachers are essential in designing this creative environment. Even those adults who do not consider themselves particularly creative can effectively nurture creativity in children. The benefits go well beyond the sheer pleasure experienced by children when making something unique and personal. Creative children tend to exude a joyful approach to living while developing problem-solving skills that will help them cope with the world around them.

Creative kids are curious kids. Enter their world, listen to their questions, and become explorers, detectives, and adventurers together. Choose things that you enjoy doing; you'll find that each experience will have a freshness to it because you will be approaching it from a different vantage point. Use the activities in this book as your stepping off point—and go further! Time with children does not have to be only structured, "quality" moments. Let children into your life. View the activities that fill your day, no matter how mundane they may seem, as opportunities to include children. This is what I term "prime time together." Prime time together is important time, valuable time, and above all, time invested in your children.

The activities in this book grew out of experiences with my own children and ideas shared with television viewers, parenting groups, neighbors, and friends. Some projects may be familiar to you, while others are brand-new. I don't claim to have invented them all; some of the best ideas are old favorites that have been handed down, adapted, and stood the test of time. But all the activities included represent a variety of good ways to enjoy some "prime time together" with your kids. That was my purpose in writing this book.

Activities for Spring

Spring is a time of beginnings, of new life. After long months of cold winter, it is a welcome sight to see crocuses and daffodils poking up through dry leaves. In cold weather climates, spring brings melting snow, puddles, and smiles on a sunny day. Even in places where there aren't mittens and woolen hats to put away, the first fresh spring breeze triggers an upsurge in spirit.

With the warmer weather, take the opportunity to get outdoors with your family and get to know one another in a new way. Observe the changes taking place in nature. Smell the earthy and damp air. Take note of returning birds, opening buds, and tiny spring flowers. Enjoy little moments together—take a short walk after the evening meal, watch a bird build a nest in your backyard, or listen to a rain shower. Give children new responsibilities while enjoying projects like planting a garden together. Even spring cleaning can be made into a fun family event with a little planning and some patience!

The activities in this section revolve around events that take place in spring. There are ideas for celebrating Easter, May Day, and Mother's and Father's Day, along with fun activities for other spring days. If you live in a cold climate, try "forced-bloom branches" to get a

headstart on spring. You can also grow a village in a saucer to bring spring to your table in time for Easter. There are egg decorating activities for every level of ability, including those that will help young children with their small motor skills. Officially welcome spring and take time to let neighbors and friends know how special they are with May Day baskets. Help kids to thank Mom or Dad with personally made gifts for Mother's or Father's Day.

As you put away winter gear and bring out raincoats and umbrellas, may spring symbolize for you a new beginning and a time for creating family traditions that will be looked forward to every year when the warm breezes blow.

Egg decorating

If you shy away from decorating Easter eggs with commercially prepared dyes, the following activities are for you! Even young children can make egg masterpieces without too much mess, but the fun is in doing them together! If you wish to keep the eggs from year to year, it is best to use blown eggs. They are more fragile than hard-boiled eggs, but when the holiday is over, you can pack them away in an empty egg carton for next year. For health reasons, do not eat hard-boiled eggs that have not been refrigerated, and do not eat them if they are sprayed with acrylic.

To blow out the contents of a raw egg: poke a hole at each end of the egg with a darning needle. Twist the needle around inside the egg until the yoke is broken. Then blow hard through the hole on top, collecting the contents of the egg in a small dish. (Plan on a few broken eggs as your kids giggle their way through the fun.) Rinse out the eggshells and allow them to air dry thoroughly before decorating.

Spongeware eggs

You will need: several eggs (blown or hard-boiled)
brown, green, blue tempera or acrylic paint
3 paper cups (one for each paint color)
small pieces of sponge or foam
6 spring-type clothespins (one for each paint color)
egg cups
newspaper
clear spray acrylic (optional)

Add a country touch to your Easter table with these easy-to-decorate eggs.

Working on a newspaper-covered surface, place egg in egg cup. Clip a piece of sponge to a clothespin and, using the clothespin as a handle, dip the sponge lightly into a paper cup partially filled with paint. (Note: a little paint goes a long way!) Lightly dab the sponge all over the top half of the egg. Let dry. Turn egg over and repeat for bottom half. When the paint has dried completely, spray the egg with clear acrylic for a permanent finish. (This should be done by an adult. Be certain to follow the manufacturer's instructions on the can.)

Pen-designed eggs

You will need: several eggs (blown or hard-boiled)
fine-tipped felt markers in a variety of colors
clear spray acrylic
yarn or ribbon (optional)

Simple doodles and intricate designs make special additions to the eggs in your Easter basket. This is an activity for all ages!

To avoid smudges, start at the center of the egg. Draw miniature flowers, Easter symbols, colorful patterns, or whatever strikes your fancy. After the drawings are completely dry, spray with clear acrylic (best done by an adult) for a permanent finish. If you wish, glue a loop of yarn or ribbon to the top of the egg and hang them on an egg tree (see Activity 2).

Marble eggs with crayons

You will need: several eggs (blown or hard-boiled)
glass jar (pint size or larger)
hot water
crayon stubs, peeled
vegetable grater
spoon
paper towels or newspaper
empty egg carton
clear spray acrylic

Safely decorate eggs with colored wax without having to heat the wax on the stove. Kids will marvel at the results!

Grate crayons over paper towel or newspaper. The adult in charge fills jar with very hot (nearly boiling) water. Drop pinches of grated crayon into the water, and as soon as the wax begins to melt, add egg, being careful not to spill water out of jar. (Remember: water does not need to be boiling to cause a burn, especially on children's sensitive skin.) Using a spoon, twirl egg in water. The wax will make a design on the shell. When you are satisfied with the design, carefully remove the egg and place it in an upside-down egg carton to prevent smearing. Let it dry. Experiment with different color combinations. Refill jar with clean hot water for each egg. When wax has dried, you may spray with clear acrylic to protect the design, following the manufacturer's instructions carefully.

Color eggs with natural dyes

You will need: several eggs (blown or hard-boiled)

various food and plant items, such as: daffodil petals, saffron, and yellow onion skins for yellow; blueberries for blue; broccoli and grass for green; walnut shells, tea, and coffee for tan (experiment to find others!)

medium-sized sauce pans (one for each color)

water

slotted spoon

newspaper

strainer

cooking oil and soft cloth

Bring back the past by dyeing your eggs the way it used to be done—with natural items straight from the kitchen and garden!

Pour ½ cup water into saucepan and add cut-up fruit, vegetable, or plant parts to water. Bring to boil and simmer until water turns the color you wish. Remove from heat and strain, reserving the water.

When water has cooled, add eggs. Allow eggs to sit in water until they turn the desired color. (Note: colors will be more subtle than those of commercial dyes.) Remove eggs with a slotted spoon and let them air dry. Polish dried eggs with a small amount of cooking oil applied to a soft cloth.

Arranged in a basket, the eggs will make a unique centerpiece for your table. During Easter dinner see if your guests can figure out the source of your egg dyes!

Make an egg tree with forced-bloom branches

You will need: garden shears, hammer
vase or jar filled with water
Easter eggs (see Activity 1),
party favors, or gift-
wrapped candy, and rib-
bon (optional)

As the days begin to warm, take a nature walk with your children and look for young, budding branches. With garden shears, clip off branches that are about 20" long. Be sure to select branches that have large buds on them. Good choices are: forsythia, lilac, tamarack, weeping willow, silver maple, and box elder. (If you are unable to find suitable branches where you live, look for forsythia branches and pussy willows at your neighborhood florist.)

Bring the branches inside and pound the clipped ends with a hammer. Arrange them in a water-filled vase or jar. Place the arrangement in a warm room and watch for young leaves to begin appearing within several days.

For fun, decorate the blooming branches by hanging blown Easter eggs on them. Or if your child has a spring birthday, tie brightly wrapped candy or party favors to the branches to make special "blooms" for the party guests to take home.

A trim behind the ears (Activity 3)

Grow sprouts in an eggshell

You will need: 1 empty eggshell with top
¼ broken off
1 egg cup or small napkin ring
3 damp cotton balls
⅛ teaspoon alfalfa seeds
fine-tipped felt markers

This miniature gardening activity is especially fun for preschool gardeners.

Set the empty eggshell in egg cup or napkin ring. Draw a face on the eggshell with colored markers (a child's self-portrait is especially fun), and set the eggshell in egg cup or napkin ring. Place damp cotton balls inside eggshell. Sprinkle seeds over the cotton and keep cotton damp. In two or three days, the seeds will begin to sprout. Put in a sunny spot. As the sprouts grow, your child can give the egg friend a "haircut." Sprinkle the nutritious clippings on a salad or add to a sandwich at lunchtime.

City planting (Activity 4)

Grow a spring village in a saucer

You will need: drainage saucer for a 10″ flowerpot
fresh potting soil
wheat berries or rye grass seed
clear plastic wrap
spray bottle filled with water
miniature items—toys, figures, animals, eggs, etc. (plastic cake decorations work well)

Kids can design their own village while nature takes care of the plant life!

Fill the drainage saucer with potting soil. Sprinkle wheat berries or rye grass seed over the entire surface of soil. Lightly spray soil with water until it is damp, not soggy. Cover with plastic wrap to retain moisture. (Remove wrap if any mold develops.) Place in indirect sunlight, and keep soil moist until seeds germinate (about 4-5 days).

After seeds have germinated, remove plastic wrap and place tray near a sunny window. Your children will be amazed to see how rapidly the green sprouts will grow. The children can create a village setting by placing small objects in the grass: miniature toys, trees made from twigs, tiny flowers cut from bright tissue paper, and figures molded from clay. Pathways can be added to the village by clipping the grass however you wish. Add miniature bunnies and eggs as Easter approaches.

A soft egg (Activity 5)

Make a Humpty Dumpty stuffed toy

You will need: butcher paper or newspaper
½ yard muslin
fabric marking pens
needle and thread or sewing machine
polyester fiber-fill stuffing
miscellaneous sewing scraps: lace, ribbon, yarn, rick-rack, buttons

Take this favorite egg character of nursery rhyme fame and make a special stuffed toy together with your child.

Enlarge pattern outline to approximately 5″ x 10″ on butcher paper or newspaper. Pin pattern to two layers of fabric, and cut out. With right sides together, sew along outside edge of fabric oval, leaving a 2″ opening at the bottom. Clip seam and turn right side out. Press. With markers, draw features for face. Add hair, a funny hat, arms, legs, and shoes by sewing scraps to body. Stuff body until firm and sew bottom opening together.

PATTERN SHAPE

OPENING

Spring delivery (Activity 6)

Celebrate May Day

You will need: (for Basket 1) ribbon, raffia, string or yarn, and empty pint-size plastic strawberry or mushroom baskets. (for Basket 2) brightly colored construction paper (9" x 12") or stiff metallic paper, stapler, stickers

Welcome spring and surprise your neighbors at the same time with May Day baskets. Making and filling the baskets is half the fun. The other half is the excitement of hanging them on unsuspecting persons' doorknobs, ringing doorbells, hiding, and waiting to see the surprise on the faces of friends who come to the door. Through all the preparation and fun, kids will experience the joy of giving of themselves to people who are important to them throughout the whole year.

Try these easy-to-make May Day baskets:

Basket 1

Weave ribbon, raffia, and yarn or string through the sides of the plastic basket. Add a handle made from wide ribbon and fill the basket with treats—candy, cookies, flowers. Add a note to tell the person that he or she is special.

Basket 2

Cut 2½" off the long end of a sheet of construction paper, to form a square. Save the piece that was cut off. Bring two adjoining sides of the square together to form a cone. Overlap edges slightly and staple cone securely. Staple the strip of paper set aside to the top of the cone to form a handle. Decorate with stickers before filling with goodies. (Note: Wallpaper remnants make a pretty alternative to construction paper.)

"My favorite teacher" (Activity 7)

Thank a teacher

You will need: construction paper
snapshot of teacher and child or school picture of child
felt-tipped markers or crayons
glue
large envelope

Many school teachers will agree that some of the most meaningful and treasured gifts they receive from their students are home-made thank-you cards. Surprise a favorite teacher at the end of the year with a special thank-you!

Fold a piece of construction paper in half to form a card. Glue a school picture or a snapshot of the teacher and your child doing an activity together to the front of the card. Have your child write a message to the teacher inside the card that details what he or she appreciated most about spending the year with the teacher. Encourage your child to be creative, perhaps putting the message in verse form. Add decorations to the card then sign it and seal it in a large envelope. It will be greatly appreciated!

Herb thyme (Activity 8)

Make an herb garden kit for Mom or Dad

You will need: inexpensive pots of herbs suitable for planting in hanging baskets (basil, chives, coriander, oregano, parsley, rosemary, and thyme are good choices)

plastic or wire hanging basket

potting soil

Here is a gift that "keeps on giving" and is perfect for Mother's Day or Father's Day.

Depending on the recipient of the gift, Mom or Dad can take the kids to a garden shop where the kids select herbs and pay for them with saved-up allowance. (This makes the gift truly theirs!) Look for inexpensive herbs in pots—small, compact plants work best—and aim for variety. Pick up an empty plastic or wire hanging basket and potting soil too. Arrange everything in a box, add a bow and a card, and the gift is complete. Kids can help Mom or Dad plant the basket after the big day, and everyone will enjoy watching the herbs grow. When a pot of soup or spaghetti sauce is cooking on the stove, kids can snip off some growing herbs to add, and liven up the evening meal!

A hands-on experience (Activity 9)

Paint a designer shirt for Mother's or Father's Day

You will need: fabric paint in several colors
sweatshirt or T-shirt in
white or light color
aluminum pie plate
waxed paper or cardboard

Kids of all ages will enjoy adding their personal touch to a gift that Mom, Dad, Grandma, or Grandpa will wear proudly.

Lay the shirt flat on a work surface. Place a piece of waxed paper or cardboard between the two layers of fabric to protect the reverse side from any paint that may soak through. Mix paint and water (10 parts paint, 1 part water) in the pie plate. Place a child's hand (palm down) in the paint and guide painted hand to shirt. Gently but firmly press the hand on the shirt, making sure that the palm and five fingers make a print. Quickly lift the hand from the shirt. Allow handprint to dry and then repeat the procedure for each child's hand, using a different color of paint for each person.

If there is an unborn baby in the family, add a "baby's footprint" to the shirt too! Make a baby's footprint by dipping the side of a child's fist in the paint and adding five tiny toes with fingerprints of paint.

For other gift ideas, add handprints to potholders, kitchen towels, or even a white hanky that Mom or Dad can frame for home or office.

Print a notepad for Mom or Dad

You will need: black felt marking pen
2″ x 6″ piece of blank paper

This charming gift adds a personal touch to Mom's or Dad's desk. The notepads are so much fun to use—and easy to do—that you'll want to print more for unique Christmas gifts for aunts and uncles too!

Have kids print the name of the person or a special greeting ("Best Dad," "Super Mom," "I Love Mom," "Dad's Do List," etc.) at the top of the piece of paper. They might also add a creative doodle or two—but leave room for Mom or Dad to add their notes! Take the paper to a local print shop and have them print a notepad with the heading appearing on each page. This will cost about $2.50 to $3.00 per notepad, depending on size, color, and quality of paper you choose. You can usually pick up the finished tablet the same day.

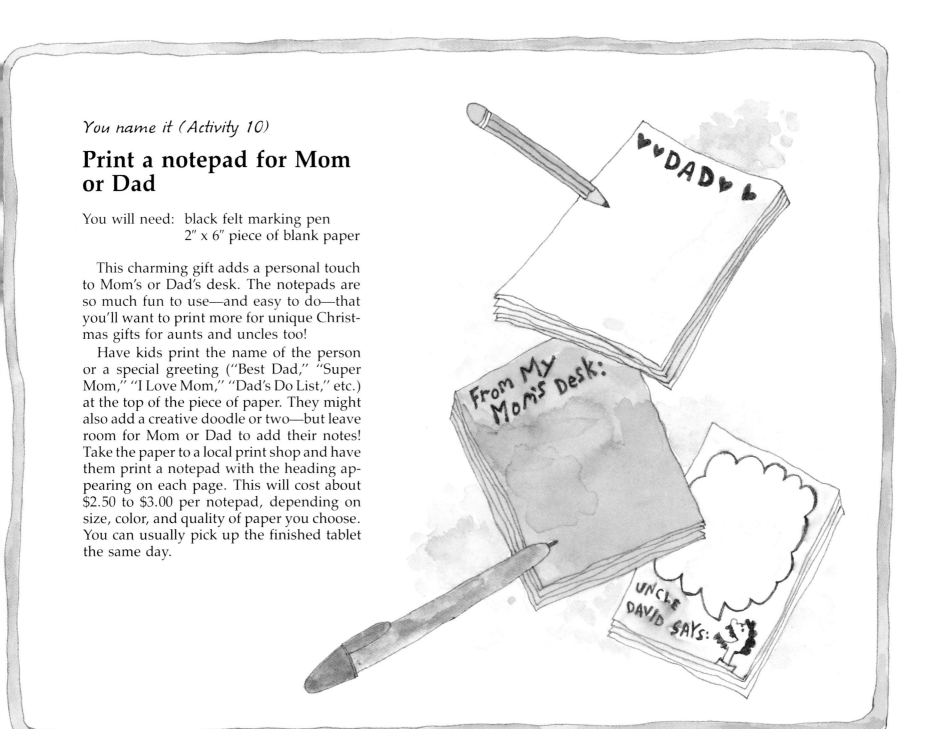

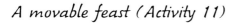

Plant a minigarden on wheels

You will need: a wheelbarrow, wagon, or wagonlike toy on wheels
potting soil
potted vegetables and plants from a nursery: parsley, beans, marigolds, pansies, petunias, begonias, etc.
vegetable or flower seeds: lettuce, radishes, marigolds, nasturtiums
small gardening tools
watering can
ice pick or similar sharp object

Don't throw away your old wagon or wheelbarrow—it can make a great container for a child's minigarden. This is an easy project for the beginning gardeners in your family, and the results are rewarding. Children can plant, weed, water, and tend their own plants without becoming overwhelmed by a big garden plot. And since the garden is portable, they can move it around the yard or deck for maximum sun exposure.

With an ice pick or sharp object, an adult should carefully poke drainage holes in the bottom of the wagon or wheelbarrow. Fill it with potting soil. Plant potted plants, keeping in mind their eventual size: put taller plants in the middle, smaller plants along the sides. Plant seeds in between plants. If there is enough room, children may plant lettuce seeds in the shape of the letter of their first name.

Water and feed the plants and seedlings regularly. (Container gardens need frequent waterings.)

Activities for Summer

When the final bell rings on the last day of school, it signals the beginning of a time to dream and pretend, to run barefoot in the warm summer sun. It also signals a time when the regular family routine is interrupted, and there is more opportunity to do things together. Whether those moments include helping a child learn how to ride a two-wheel bike, heading off on a fishing trip, or going on the annual family picnic, they are times that shape our children's lives.

Nature provides an alluring backdrop for summer outdoor activities—we can observe wildlife on a camping trip, watch our vegetable gardens grow, or just enjoy keeping up the yard. Let summer be a time for encouraging within your child a love for creation and a responsible attitude toward caring for the earth. Become a model for your child in the ways you observe the beauty of the great outdoors.

The summer months offer a host of events for families to enjoy together. You might want to attend your community's mid-summer festival or fair, listen to a concert in the park, check out what your library has to offer, or consider joining in on a community project like cleaning up a park or painting an elderly person's home. If your community doesn't have such projects, you might even band together with your neighbors and sponsor something. Get started by holding a block party to get to know the new people in your area.

You might take the opportunity to get to know your family better, too, by planning a family reunion. As families increasingly live farther apart, reunions have become important events where extended family members can become reacquainted and, in some cases, meet one another for the first time. Investigate your family's history, contact distant relatives, and invite everyone to come. Enlist the help of nearby relatives, and make the reunion as elaborate or as simple as you wish.

Summer is also the traditional time for family vacations. Let your annual vacation be a fun learning experience for everyone. Travel to a place you have never visited, far away or close to home. Before you go, read about the history of the place and take note of interesting sites along your travel route. If you don't plan to take an extended vacation, try mini-outings like a day at the zoo, a weekend camping trip, an afternoon of fishing, or even a leisurely evening bike ride. Whatever you choose to do, include the entire family in planning the activity.

This section contains many activities and ideas for enjoying summertime. The suggestions are in some cases structured ways to be "unstructured." Should a rainy day spoil your plans, there are fun art projects to do indoors that can be displayed on another day at a neighborhood art fair. So when the screen door slams, announcing the arrival of your child who declares, "I'm bored! There's nothing to do," consider an activity you can do together. Even if it's only sipping lemonade under a shady tree for a few minutes, you and your child will be enjoying prime time together.

Bubble, bubble, toil, and—fun
(Activity 12)

Make the best bubble brew

You will need: 1 cup Joy liquid dishwashing detergent
2 cups warm water
3-4 tablespoons glycerine (found at drugstores)
1 teaspoon sugar
large plastic container
"found" bubble makers (see below)

Blowing and chasing bubbles is great entertainment for all ages. Here's the perfect recipe that will guarantee spectacular bubbles whether you blow them or wave your bubble maker like a wand.

Gently stir all ingredients together in a big plastic container. Then be a detective in your home and hunt for clever, unbreakable items that will make super bubbles. To get you started, try: plastic six-pack beverage holders, biscuit cutters, paper cups, plastic coat hangers, antique rug beaters, straws, and funnels. Dip your bubble makers into the brew and either blow through them or wave them in the air. If you want to save your bubble brew for another time, cover the plastic container with a tight fitting lid and store.

Ship shape! (Activity 13)

Make boats from nature and recycled materials

You will need: (for nature boats) reeds, bark, feathers, leaves

(for recycled boats) fast-food hamburger and french fry containers, drinking straw

Nature boats

Take a reed that is about ½″ wide and 6″ long. With your thumb nail, slit an opening 1″ long near the wide end (don't extend the slit all the way to the end). Slip 1½″ of the narrow end of the reed through the opening to make a loop for a sail. For bark boats, poke a feather or a strong leaf into the middle of a small piece of bark. (The fun is in the hunting for feathers and just the right piece of bark!)

Recycled boats

Before you toss your fast food containers, set them afloat! (But be sure to discard the boat in a proper receptacle when it's time to go home.) First, cut the french fry carton in the shape of a sail. Make two slits in it—one near the top, the other near the bottom. Insert the drinking straw through the slits. Then poke the straw through the middle of the lid from a hamburger container to complete the boat. For fun, send it adrift with secret messages tucked inside.

BIG BURGER

Bring home the beach (Activity 14)

Create beach souvenirs to take home

You will need: 1 box of plaster of Paris
(available from paint and
hardware stores)
empty coffee can or plastic
ice cream pail
paint stirring sticks
paper cup
paper clips

Bring along a carton of plaster of Paris, a paper cup, and a coffee can the next time you go to the beach, and come home with a unique piece of art. If your kids have made plaster handprints in school, they'll be familiar with the "how-tos."

Scoop out a design at least 2" deep in the wet sand. (Be sure the tide won't be coming in soon!) Connecting areas should also be 2" wide, to keep your project from breaking. This will be your mold. Decorate it with natural objects you collect on the beach: shells, rocks, sticks, bark, weeds. You may also make a mold with a toy such as plastic fish or crab. When your mold is complete, mix the plaster of Paris. Pour one or two cups of lake or sea water into the coffee can or pail. Add the powdered plaster and stir. The mixture should be smooth and thick (but pourable). Do not overstir, however, as this causes the mixture to set up too quickly and weakens the final product. Immediately pour the mixture into your sand mold, spreading it evenly to all areas with a stick, if necessary.

To make a hanger for your project, poke a paper clip halfway into the plaster at the center top. If the project is large, you may wish to position two paper clips evenly spaced from each side.

Allow the plaster to harden (1 to 1½ hours, depending on the size of the project), and then carefully remove the plaster souvenir from the sand. Dispose of leftover plaster and coffee can properly. Take a picture of your pleased kids holding their creations before you transport them home.

MOLD
SCOOPED
OUT OF →
SAND

Make a water scope

You will need: ½ gallon paper milk carton, washed and dry
heavy plastic wrap
1 heavy rubber band
masking tape or wide plastic tape

Are your kids budding marine biologists? The summertime can bring them into closer contact with fascinating living things in water; whether along the seashore, by a lake or in a stream, pond or creek. Arouse their curiosity for water life by making this water scope together. When your kids first peek below the surface of the water with their own water scope, you're sure to hear squeals of "Come here, quick, look!" Even if it's only a speck of tree bark floating by, your kids will feel like young Cousteaus making important discoveries.

Cut off the top and bottom of the milk carton. Place plastic wrap over the open bottom end, bringing it up over the outside of the carton and over the top opening. Tape the wrap to the inside of the carton at the top. Wrap a rubber band around the bottom of the carton to secure the plastic wrap. Slowly place it in the water. Hold it still and look through the plastic for something interesting.

Make a moss wreath

You will need: 1 purchased or homemade straw or grapevine wreath

natural materials gathered from a walk in the woods or countryside: moss, lichen, bark (do not pick these materials off trees; collect them from the ground along your path), pinecones, small branches with colorful leaves (see Activity 36 for directions on preserving leaves)

glue gun or wood glue

6" length of medium gauge wire

newspaper

ribbon (optional)

Using a premade or purchased wreath as a base, your school-age children can make unusual moss wreaths to adorn a wall in your living room or decorate your front door.

Shake off any mud or debris from materials you have gathered and let them dry. Lay everything out on a newspaper-covered work surface. An adult should apply the glue, if you use a glue gun, while the children arrange the moss and lichen, pressing it into the glue. Be very careful when using a glue gun, to avoid nasty burns. For variety, wrap several pieces of bark around the wreath, and attach pinecones and leaves for color. Add a ribbon, if desired. Make a loop with the wire and attach it to the back of the wreath. When the wreath is completely dry, it is ready to hang.

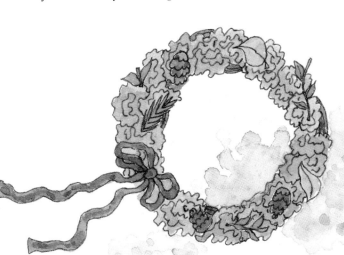

In the beginning . . . (Activity 17)

Interview a relative and learn about your family's history

You will need: a tape recorder or video
camera (check the batter-
ies to be certain it will
function properly)

an empty cassette tape or
videotape (You might
want an extra one, just in
case. Use cassette tapes
that are no longer than 30
minutes on each side;
longer ones tend to dis-
tort voices.)

relatives to interview

a quiet place

Preserve a bit of family history on cassette or videotape. This is a fun activity for a family reunion.

Taking time to interview a relative is worth every minute. Children can pretend they are reporters and prepare questions in advance. Adults may prefer an informal conversation. Everyone will enjoy finding out the things that make your family unique. A bonus to this activity is the relationships that may develop between children and older adults. Such contact helps young people form positive attitudes toward aging and the passing of time.

Prepare a list of questions before the interview. Open-ended questions are best, for they stimulate ideas and trigger memories.

What is your birthdate? Where were you born?

What were your parents' and grandparents' names?

What did they do for a living?

What one special thing do you remember about each of them?

Where did you go to school? What did you like most about school? What did you like least?

What was your favorite activity as a child?

Describe the house (or town) you grew up in.

What was your most memorable birthday?

What made you afraid when you were a child?

How did you meet your spouse? Describe your first date.

What has changed most in your lifetime?

If you could live your life over, what would you do differently?

At the beginning of the interview, record the date, location, and names of the people. Label the cassette. Once you start asking questions, let the conversation develop on its own. You may also wish to ask questions about specific old photos or heirlooms (this works especially well if you are videotaping). Use an atlas to find the cities, states, or countries from which your ancestors came. Jot down a family recipe that has been handed down, and prepare it for a special occasion.

Family ties (Activity 18)

Make a family tree centerpiece

You will need: bare tree branches, spray painted, if you wish

plaster of Paris (available at paint and hardware stores)

large plastic margarine tub or plastic ice cream pail

decorative paper or tissue

ribbon

wooden or plastic curtain loops

scissors

glue or tape

Include in your invitations to a family reunion a request that each person bring a snapshot of himself or herself. Before the actual day of the reunion, prepare the tree part of the centerpiece. Mix the plaster of Paris in the margarine tub or pail, according to the instructions on the package. As the plaster begins to harden, stick in the branches. Arrange them as you wish, and hold them in place for several minutes until they no longer require support. Allow the plaster to set for at least two hours. (When cleaning up, do not pour excess plaster down the drain; it will harden.) Cover the container with bright tissue paper and ribbon.

On the day of the reunion, invite relatives to complete the centerpiece by gluing or taping their photos to the backs of the curtain loops. String some ribbon through the hangers on the top of the loops and tie them to the branches. When all the relatives have arrived, use the centerpiece as the focus of a get-to-know-one-another game.

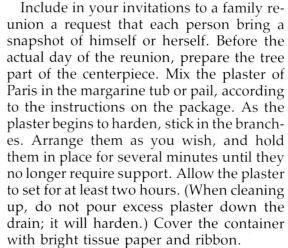

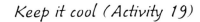

Create an ice cream watermelon dessert

You will need: 1 plastic lettuce crisper or other oval shaped mold
1 quart lime sherbet
1 quart strawberry or raspberry ice cream or sherbet (if using ice cream, do not use brands with fruit chunks in it)
1 cup semisweet chocolate chips
lime slices, mint leaves, strawberries, fruit juice, and sparkling mineral water (optional)

Kids will have fun making this whimsical dessert from their favorite ingredients. Enjoy the treat at summer gatherings of relatives and friends. You can even eat the seeds in this watermelon!

Spread lime sherbet along the sides of the lettuce crisper, making a layer about 1" to 1½" thick along all sides and leaving a cavity in the center. (This is the rind.) Kids will enjoy smooshing the ice cream around—watch that their hands don't get too cold. Fill the center cavity with strawberry or raspberry ice cream, adding chocolate chips (the seeds) as you go along. Chill in freezer for at least six hours. When you're ready to serve, place a warm towel around the mold until the ice cream slips out of the bowl. Place on its side on a serving platter. (It should resemble a watermelon half.) Garnish with lime slices, mint leaves, and strawberries. To serve, slice off individual servings, just as you would with real watermelon. For a healthy beverage to go with the dessert, add fresh fruit juice to sparkling mineral water—a nice alternative to sugary soft drinks.

33

Prepare school-age children for a major trip

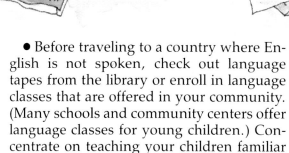

Summer is the traditional vacation time for families, and to really enjoy the time together, some planning is in order. The more well-planned the vacation, the less tension there will be when you actually hit the road. Vacation planning should include the entire family—kids too. The following tips will help you prepare for your best trip ever.

● Arriving unprepared in a new city or country can be intimidating and frightening to children, as well as to adults. Check out books, pamphlets, and magazines from your local library, and spend time together learning about your destination. Pinpoint some particular landmark or attraction along the way that will be of special interest to children.

● Have children write to the Chamber of Commerce or tourist bureau of the place you will be visiting. Encourage them to ask for helpful information such as attractions they might enjoy and special events that might be taking place during the time you will be visiting. Children love receiving their own "travel" mail.

● Before traveling to a country where English is not spoken, check out language tapes from the library or enroll in language classes that are offered in your community. (Many schools and community centers offer language classes for young children.) Concentrate on teaching your children familiar and useful phrases.

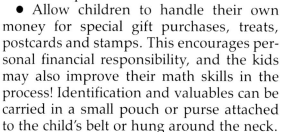

● Allow children to handle their own money for special gift purchases, treats, postcards and stamps. This encourages personal financial responsibility, and the kids may also improve their math skills in the process! Identification and valuables can be carried in a small pouch or purse attached to the child's belt or hung around the neck.

● Let your children help pack for the trip. Personal items they choose to take along can be of comfort to them in an unfamiliar place.

As you plan with your children, share their enthusiasm, anticipate their questions, enjoy their excited expressions, and, once on your way, take many pictures to capture the memories!

Keep in touch (Activity 21)

Pretravel diary

You will need: 4" x 6" index cards (one for each child for each day you are gone)

It's not uncommon nowadays for Mom and Dad to take a trip without kids. Parents may accompany each other on a business trip, take off to a foreign country for a number of days, or just have a weekend getaway together. To involve the kids and keep them aware of your travel plans, try this activity. It really works—and best of all, it encourages exchanges of experiences once the trip is over and you are back home.

On one side of an index card, print the date of your first day away and briefly state what you intend to do. Add a personal comment if you wish, for example: "I arrive in Brussels today. I love their french fries. The Belgians eat french fries with mayonnaise. Isn't that funny?" Make a similar card for each day you will be gone. Clip the cards together. Instruct the person who is caring for your children to give each a card to read each day at breakfast. In the evening the children should write about their day on the backside of their card. (If the child is too young to write, he or she can dictate the events to an older sibling or adult.)

When you return from your trip, sit down with your kids and read through the cards. You can catch up on what you missed while gone, and they can relive your vacation!

Mon. July 11

Dear Gordy,
  Tonight we are going to the New York Symphony. I wonder how many violinists we'll see.
  Love, Mom

July 10

Today I baked cookies. I'm saving one for you.

Mileage countdown bags for in the car

You will need: 3 or 4 paper lunch bags for
each child
string or ribbon
felt-tipped markers
inexpensive toys that can be
used in the car: books,
stickers, etc.; jumprope
for a rest stop
snack items: small packages
of peanuts, raisins, or
fruit snacks, fruit, gran-
ola bars, rice cakes, boxes
of fruit juice, packages of
gum, etc.

Even though this activity requires a little extra effort on the part of Mom or Dad, it will be worth it once you are on the road. Not only does it curb the whining question, "Are we almost there?", but it encourages good behavior as kids anticipate opening their next mileage bag. Older children will be able to trace your route on the map, and predict when the mileage bag will come, and they may take a keener interest in map reading and geography.

Before your trip, print the name of each child on the outside of three or four lunch bags. Looking at your planned route on the map, determine points where you think the kids will be ready for a snack, toy, game, book, etc. (Every 50 miles or so seems to work best for school-age children.) Write the number of miles you have traveled or the name of a city you will arrive at on each of the bags. Once you are traveling, the children will receive the appropriate bag at the spot you have noted.

Put an item in each bag, making sure that each child receives the same type of treat at the same time. For example, put one juice box in each 100-mile bag. Try to judge when certain items would be appropriate and helpful (evenly space out food items and toys, perhaps).

Tie the bags shut with string or ribbon and place in a basket or box that will sit next to you during the trip. Explain the mileage game at the beginning of the trip, and watch the miles fly by!

Alphabet diary car game

You will need: 1 small 50-page notebook
1 large zip-lock style plastic bag
a pen or pencil
crayons or felt-tipped markers (optional)

Here's a car activity that won't bore your children because they will be too busy looking for things!

Prior to beginning your trip, have the children write their names, the date of departure, and your destination on the cover of their notebooks. Then, at the top of each page, have them print one letter of the alphabet, beginning with A and ending with Z. (An older sibling or Mom or Dad could help younger children.) Store the notebook and pencil in the plastic bag.

Along the way, the children should look for special landmarks or items of interest and write the names of the landmarks or items next to the appropriate letters in the notebook. For example, *barn* would go on the page with B at the top. Under the word, have them draw a picture of the item.

After reaching your destination, encourage the children to continue filling in the blank pages. Extra pages can serve as a diary of activities you and your family take part in during the rest of your vacation. Once home, the children may wish to color their pictures to complete a unique souvenir of their trip. The entire family will enjoy looking at one another's diaries, and you may want to tuck them away to be enjoyed in future years.

Miles of fun (Activity 24)

Keeping young children busy in the car

You will need: magnetic-backed letters, numbers, and toys that you may have around the house
stainless steel cookie sheet or cake pan with lid
zip-lock style plastic bag
self-adhesive-backed magnetic strips (optional)

Gather all the magnetic-backed toys your kids play with (don't forget those stuck to your refrigerator) or create some of your own by attaching self-stick magnets to the backs of small toys, and put them in a plastic bag for the trip. Once on your way, your child can spell words or create pictures on the cookie sheet or cake pan with the magnets. An alternative to magnets are vinyl shapes and forms that stick easily to the side car windows and can be removed and stored in a jiffy. (Do not put on rear windows, as this can obstruct the view of the driver.)

For older children, you may want to check into purchasing travel games such as checkers that have magnetic-backed pieces for easy playing.

200 MILES TO CALIFORNIA

No postage necessary (Activity 25)

Keep a travel journal on postcards

You will need: postcards (collected as you
visit places)
paper punch
metal ring (found at stationery stores)

Keeping a travel diary often can be un-
realistic for most young children, especially
after a tiring day of travel. An easy way to
keep a record of the day's activities and
places visited is to collect picture postcards
as the trip progresses. When the children
have a few quiet moments after lunch, for
example, they can jot down on the backside
of the postcard the date and what they did
at the place pictured. As they collect the
postcards, punch a hole in the top left corner
and attach them together on a metal ring
found at stationery stores. Months and
years after the trip, the kids will enjoy looking through the postcards and reading their
notes.

Front-yard gallery (Activity 26)

Organize a neighborhood art fair

You will need: art projects gathered from the children in your area

construction paper for making tickets, or purchased roll of tickets

paper for posters and flyers

clothesline and clothespins

butcher paper

crayons or felt-tipped markers

cookies, lemonade, popcorn

paper cups, napkins

cashier's box with extra change

face paints (see Activity 42)

balloons, streamers

tape player and music cassettes

card tables or picnic tables (for display purposes)

Are you wondering what to do with all the art projects your children have brought home from school that are overflowing from your closets and refrigerator door? Consider holding a neighborhood art fair! You can even sell the masterpieces, along with refreshments, and donate the money to a local charity or community organization. (Be sure to keep the prices very reasonable.)

This activity takes some coordinating on the part of adults and children. Contact your neighbors and set up activities they wish to be involved with: setting up art displays, working at the fair, cleaning up afterward, making posters, selling tickets, providing refreshments (cookies, popcorn, lemonade), face painting, putting on puppet shows or other entertainment—the more the merrier! Then, gather all the art projects you can find and encourage your neighbors to do the same. Publicize the event with posters (made by kids) or photocopied flyers that state the time, place, and date. (A good time is between 4 and 7 P.M. or on a weekend, so working parents can attend.)

On the day of the art fair, set up your displays along your sidewalk, in the front yard, in your driveway, or on your deck or porch (depending on the size of the fair and the weather). String clothesline between trees and poles, and hang paintings, drawings, and some crafts with clothespins. Display sculpture, jewelry, painted rocks, and the like on a picnic table or card table. Set up the refreshments center and a ticket sales booth. You may wish to include a "Permanent Collection" display of artwork that will not be offered for sale. Decorate the area with streamers and balloons and play music to liven the atmosphere. Put up posters at places where entertainment and face painting will take place. For toddlers, roll out a long sheet of butcher paper on the ground and place crayons or colored markers next to the paper. The little Picassos can doodle on the paper while the older kids enjoy the event.

As people arrive at the fair, they may purchase tickets to be used for buying treats, purchasing art, face painting, and viewing performances. When the fair is over, have designated helpers clean up, return unsold art, and count the proceeds. Decide on a charity or community service that would benefit from the money, and deliver it with several of the children. Submit a photo or two of the event to your community newspaper—the event just might appear in print!

Just in case you don't think you have enough artwork for such a fair, consider including the following activities as artwork!

Stuffed acetate shapes

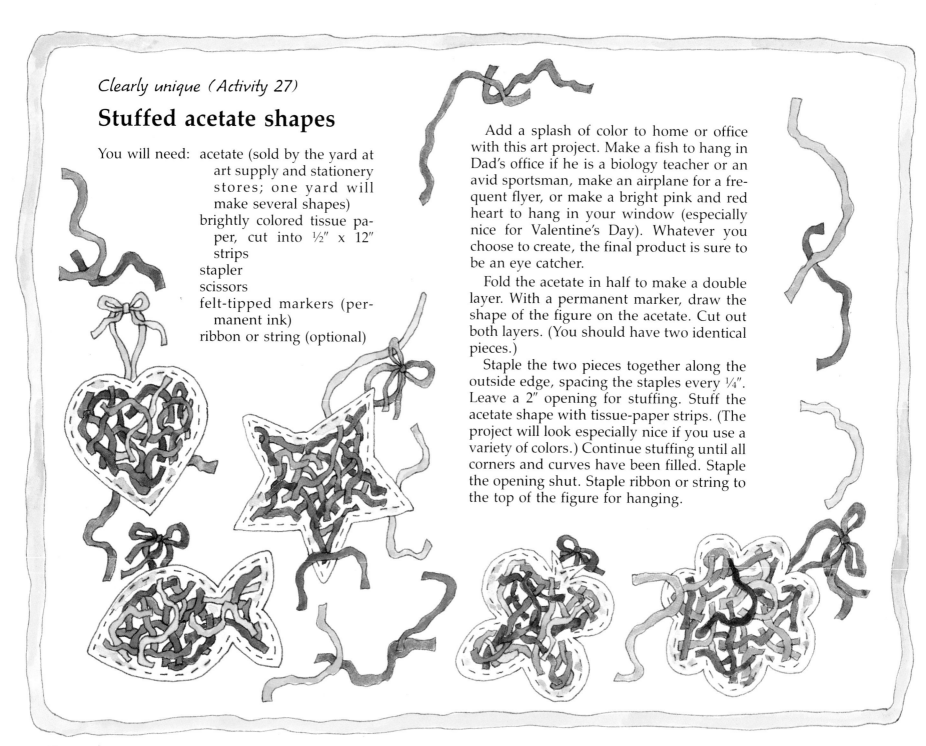

You will need: acetate (sold by the yard at art supply and stationery stores; one yard will make several shapes)

brightly colored tissue paper, cut into ½" x 12" strips

stapler

scissors

felt-tipped markers (permanent ink)

ribbon or string (optional)

Add a splash of color to home or office with this art project. Make a fish to hang in Dad's office if he is a biology teacher or an avid sportsman, make an airplane for a frequent flyer, or make a bright pink and red heart to hang in your window (especially nice for Valentine's Day). Whatever you choose to create, the final product is sure to be an eye catcher.

Fold the acetate in half to make a double layer. With a permanent marker, draw the shape of the figure on the acetate. Cut out both layers. (You should have two identical pieces.)

Staple the two pieces together along the outside edge, spacing the staples every ¼". Leave a 2" opening for stuffing. Stuff the acetate shape with tissue-paper strips. (The project will look especially nice if you use a variety of colors.) Continue stuffing until all corners and curves have been filled. Staple the opening shut. Staple ribbon or string to the top of the figure for hanging.

Tie dye in reverse

You will need: 100% cotton, colored T-shirts, jeans, or socks
liquid chlorine bleach
rubber bands and string
large bucket
rubber gloves
wooden spoon or stirring stick

This reverse technique was discovered after I accidentally spilled some bleach on my son's wadded-up navy socks. After experimenting with grubby T-shirts and jeans, we decided the process and results were just as fun as traditional tie dyeing. And we added some pizzazz and character to otherwise worn-out clothing along the way! For safety's sake, kids should do the tying, while an adult handles the bleach and water solution.

Have kids scrunch portions of the fabric into little balls, binding them tightly with rubber bands. Or, fold the fabric accordion-style and tie it tightly together at intervals with string.

An adult wearing rubber gloves then places the tied garments into the bleach solution—a bucket of hot water plus two cups of liquid chlorine bleach. Stir the garments occasionally, keeping an eye on the color changes taking place. Add more bleach, if necessary. When satisfied with the look (the fabric will appear more faded when dry), transfer the garments to your washing machine, add the normal amount of laundry detergent, and run the regular wash and rinse cycle. Then remove the strings and rubber bands and allow the garments to dry.

RUBBER BANDS

TIGHTLY TIED STRING

Nature's palette (Activity 29)

Make a picture with colors from nature

You will need: a variety of plants and flowers, such as grass, leaves, dandelions, geraniums, etc.
crayons or felt-tipped markers

The next time your children are drawing a picture at the picnic table in your backyard, acquaint them with colors that come from growing plants and flowers. Pick some flowers from your garden, choose some blades of grass, add a leaf or two, and rub them on drawing paper to see what colors they make. Experiment with different plants and different colors to make an interesting picture. To emphasize particular objects in your picture, such as trees, flowers, houses, or people, draw an outline with crayons or markers and then fill in with nature's colors. Try dandelion yellow, grass green, and geranium pink for starters.

Note: Since some plants or parts of plants can be toxic, closely supervise children and do not allow them to put anything in their mouths. Scrub hands thoroughly when finished.

Wad a picture! (Activity 30)

Create pinched-tissue art

You will need: several sheets of brightly colored tissue paper, cut into ½" x 16" strips

12" x 16" white art paper or construction paper

paper cup

white school glue (water soluble)

artist paintbrush

newspaper

sequins, glitter, small beads (optional)

This is perfect for a preschooler's first art project!

Pour a small amount of white glue into the paper cup (enough to cover the bottom) and add about ¼ cup water. Mix thoroughly. Cover your work surface with newspaper, and lay out white paper, glue mixture, tissue-paper strips and paintbrush.

Using the paintbrush, the children should "paint" the glue solution on the art paper—the more glue, the better—then crumple up strips of tissue paper and press them onto the art paper. Encourage them to use a variety of colors and arrange the wads of paper in whatever fashion they wish. Add more glue solution whenever needed. Once satisfied with the picture, set it aside to dry. Display the finished art project at home for the whole family to enjoy, or frame it for the office as a colorful reminder of your child.

For a variation of this project, sprinkle sequins, brightly colored beads, and glitter on the glue—you'll have fireworks going in all directions!

45

Outdoor painting activity for toddlers

You will need: clean paintbrushes
empty paint pail or plastic bucket
one-step booster stool
painter's cap
soap and water

The next time your toddler wants to "help"—as in wash the car or paint the garage door with you—try these "painting" ideas. They will give you a chance to spend some time with your child and get some projects done, too. Cleanup is a snap!

When you are painting, fill an empty paint can or pail with water. Give your kids clean paintbrushes, put painters' caps on their heads, and let them "water" paint the side of the house. The water makes the paint on the house look a different color until it dries. Use one-step booster stools so toddlers have a "ladder" too.

When you are washing the car, fill a cleaning bucket with suds and water. Let the children paint the soapy water on the car—they especially like to work on the tires.

Just for fun: When your kids say they have nothing to do, suggest they take a paintbrush, dip it into some mud, and draw pictures or write words on the sidewalk. It can be hosed off later or erased with the next rain shower.

Let your fingers do the drawing
(Activity 32)

Make your own finger paints

You will need: 3 tablespoons sugar
½ cup cornstarch
2 cups cold water
food coloring (variety of colors)
soap flakes or liquid dish-washing detergent
medium-sized saucepan
muffin tin or 4 or 5 small cups
freezer paper
old shirts for paint smocks

Though most parents leave finger painting to preschool and kindergarten classes, there may be moments when even adults have the urge to get their hands in the "stuff" and enjoy this simple art form at home with their children.

Pick up some freezer paper at the grocery store; it's cheaper than the special finger paint paper, and it works just as well. One roll will make a great many masterpieces. Note: When painting, use the shiny side of the freezer paper.

Then prepare your finger paints using this recipe: Mix 3 tablespoons sugar and ½ cup cornstarch together in a medium saucepan over low heat. Add 2 cups cold water and continue stirring until the mixture is thick. Remove from heat. Divide the mixture up into four or five portions, spooning them into sections of a muffin tin or small cups. Add a drop or two of food coloring (a different color for each cup) and a pinch of soap flakes or a drop of detergent to each portion. Stir and let cool. You're ready to paint! If you have paints left over, they may be stored, covered, in an airtight container.

by Ricky

Frame-up (Activity 33)

Three easy ways to display children's art

You will need: mat board (available at craft or art stores)
art clips (available at office supply stores)
wooden embroidery hoop
second-hand frames (check the garage sales!)

If your refrigerator door is overloaded with your children's works of art, you may want to try some of these inexpensive, easy-to-do framing ideas for attractive displays on your walls. Before you begin, remember to date and write your child's name on the back of all the projects you save.

1. For small- to medium-sized drawings, use a wooden embroidery hoop purchased at fabric or craft stores. Center the smaller hoop under the art and bring the hoops together as you would with needlework. Trim off the extra paper around the edge, and hang on the wall.

2. To display a larger drawing (up to 8½" x 11"), purchase mat board. A craft or art store will cut the matting to the exact size of the art, or you can buy precut, standard-size matting. Center the drawing behind the mat board and clip them together at the top with colorful spring clips available from office supply stores. Place the matted art on a plate rack for displaying on your hutch, mantel, or bookcase. Because the art is attached to the matting with clips, the picture may be easily removed when a new drawing is brought home to take its place.

3. Renovate second-hand frames you pick up at garage sales. Clean the wood, reglue, and paint, if necessary. Be careful when cleaning; watch for sharp edges and loose nails. If you paint the frame, use left-over wall or stencil paint from the room in which the art will hang. (Frames that blend with the wall will draw more attention to the art piece itself.) Take your frame to a frame or craft shop where you can get matting cut to size. Mount the artwork on sturdy cardboard (you can purchase special mount board if you wish), add glass or plexiglass to the front, and hang it where it will get the most raves!

Activities for Fall

Seeing the yellow school buses resume their routes in September is a sure sign of fall. As your child waves good-bye and boards the bus on the first day of school, you are instantly aware that a new schedule and life-style will affect your family's life for the next nine months.

Fall is naturally a busy time, with school, church, and other organizational activities starting up again. Each family member reacts differently to a new routine and season. Some may take the opportunity to get organized after a lazy summer. In my family, that means sneaking into the kids' rooms and throwing out a lot of "stuff" they have accumulated throughout the summer. Even though I try to be clever about it, sooner or later one of the kids notices something is missing. It may be only a smashed, worn-out egg carton my son used for a tackle box in June, but I find myself stammering, trying to come up with a reasonable excuse my four-year-old will accept. The best way to make amends is to suggest we get a new carton and go for a walk to collect treasures the autumn season brings us.

It seems that in the fall, families need to plan their schedules carefully, allowing time for the many demands of meetings and games and music lessons and on and on. When planning, families also need to remember to schedule some time together, some time for fun. As parents, we might want to pledge to spend time each day helping our kids with their school work or reading to them or telling a story. Even raking the yard can be a fun family event with a special treat at the end.

This section is full of activities you can enjoy out-of-doors in the crisp autumn air. Spend a day in the country picking apples for an apple wreath, collect some fall leaves and weeds for a centerpiece, or simply enjoy the beauty of the changing world around you. You might find a pumpkin patch along the way where kids can pick their own for Halloween fun, if your family celebrates Halloween. Also included are activities for Thanksgiving, a time when we stop to give thanks for all that we have.

Fall is a good time to take inventory of our homes and our lives. As we clean out the remnants of summer and bring out fall clothes, we can also take stock of the relationships we have with our children. The new fall schedule gives us the opportunity to establish some family routines that can last the year through.

Make a summer memory collage

You will need: an assortment of favorite summer souvenirs and "finds," (ticket stubs, postcards, travel brochures, maps, snapshots, etc.)

18" x 24" poster frame (available at discount stores, department stores, and photo shops)

construction paper or poster board cut to the size of the frame

glue or Plasti-tak adhesive putty (available at office supply and stationery stores)

glass cleaner and clean rag

Whether it's stashing away ticket stubs from the baseball game or unusual leaves found at the park, kids love collecting things. Here's an easy way to put those memories on display instead of letting them collect dust under the bed!

Place the poster frame on a flat surface, and remove the clips and glass. Wash glass with glass cleaner and set aside. Place the construction paper or poster board on the frame backing. Arrange the souvenir items, fixing them to the paper with a dot of glue or Plasti-tak. When complete, place glass over the collage and attach metal clips. Hang the finished collage in the child's bedroom or on your family room wall. The memories of summer will last far into the cold days of winter! And because the frame snaps apart, you can reuse it year after year, replacing old memories with new.

Sticks and stones (Activity 35)

Display a rock collection

You will need: a clear glass or crystal vase
with a base at least 3″ in
diameter
rocks that are about ¾″ to 1″
in diameter
dried weeds or flowers

Are you tired of tripping over your child's rock collection? Do miniboulders turn up in the strangest places around your home? Consider putting some of the favorite rocks on display in this attractive and *contained* fashion.

Carefully place rocks into the vase, stacking them until they fill about ⅓ of the container. Add dried weeds and flowers and place the arrangement on a table, mantel, or hutch—wherever it will get the most attention. Children will enjoy pointing out their favorite rocks and telling stories about where they were found. If you wish, cover the rocks with water to make them shine, and in the evenings place a candle nearby. The little "gems" will sparkle!

Preserve leaves with glycerine and water

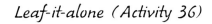

You will need: a variety of colorful fall
leaves
newspaper
lightweight hammer
(child's toy hammer
works well)
large jar
glycerine (available from
drug stores)
hot water

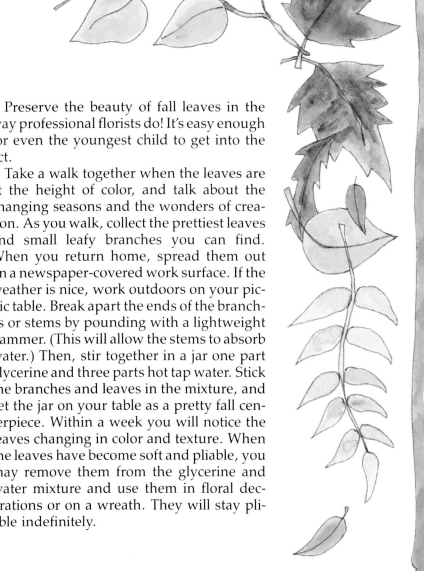

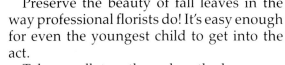

Preserve the beauty of fall leaves in the way professional florists do! It's easy enough for even the youngest child to get into the act.

Take a walk together when the leaves are at the height of color, and talk about the changing seasons and the wonders of creation. As you walk, collect the prettiest leaves and small leafy branches you can find. When you return home, spread them out on a newspaper-covered work surface. If the weather is nice, work outdoors on your picnic table. Break apart the ends of the branches or stems by pounding with a lightweight hammer. (This will allow the stems to absorb water.) Then, stir together in a jar one part glycerine and three parts hot tap water. Stick the branches and leaves in the mixture, and set the jar on your table as a pretty fall centerpiece. Within a week you will notice the leaves changing in color and texture. When the leaves have become soft and pliable, you may remove them from the glycerine and water mixture and use them in floral decorations or on a wreath. They will stay pliable indefinitely.

Waxed elegance (Activity 37)

Preserve leaves with wax

You will need: a variety of colorful fall
    leaves
    waxed paper
    iron and ironing board
    newspaper

An alternative to preserving leaves in water and glycerine (see Activity 36) is to wax them. Collect your favorite leaves from a fall jaunt and wax them before they dry, wrinkle, and crumble away.

Cover your ironing board with several layers of newspaper (to protect the surface from the wax), then place a sheet of waxed paper on top. Arrange the leaves on the waxed paper and cover them with a second sheet of waxed paper. Cover with one layer of newspaper and place iron (set at medium heat) on top. Hold iron in place for 30 seconds. Continue this process until all areas of the waxed paper have been heated and the wax has melted sufficiently. Lift off the newspaper and top layer of waxed paper. Remove the leaves. They should be waxed enough to retain their shape. Arrange them in a copper pot, stoneware crock, vase, or even a scooped-out pumpkin or gourd.

MED.

NEWSPAPER →

WAXED PAPER →

LEAVES →

WAXED PAPER →

NEWSPAPERS →

The autumn leaves drift on my window (Activity 38)

Window stenciling with leaves

You will need: a variety of leaves (different sizes and shapes)
orange, yellow, red, and brown tempera or acrylic paint
pieces of sponge
spring-type clothespins
masking tape
paper cups (one for each paint color)
newspaper
brown, red, or black crayon

To add fall colors to your windows, try this stenciling technique that uses real leaves for the patterns. Collect leaves in a variety of shapes and sizes, and arrange them on your table in the way you want them to appear in stenciled form on your window. Attach rolled pieces of masking tape to the backsides of the leaves and stick them on the window. (Make certain the leaves lie flat against the pane.)

Pour a small amount of paint into the paper cups; blend colors for interesting shades. Clip sponge piece to the clothespin and dab lightly into the paint. Blot the sponge on newspaper to absorb excess paint, and then lightly dab the sponge around the edge of the leaves. Change paint colors as you go along, using a new piece of sponge for each color. When the paint is dry, carefully remove the leaves from the window. Draw in veins and outline the pattern of the leaf with crayon, if you wish. When you are ready to remove the leaf patterns from the window, wash gently with window cleaner and a soft cloth.

Make an apple wreath

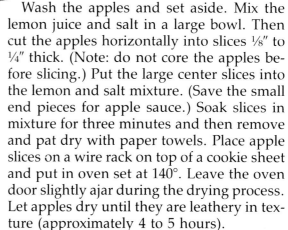

You will need: 20-25 apples
2 cups reconstituted lemon juice
2 tablespoons salt
wire hanger and wire cutter
paper towels
wire cooling rack and cookie sheet
large bowl
knife
ribbon
glue, cinnamon sticks, baby's breath, or bunches of wheat (optional)

Fall is apple season! If you live near an apple orchard, begin this activity by visiting the orchard and picking your own apples. You'll be amazed by the variety of tastes, textures, and uses of apples. The trip is an activity in itself!

Wash the apples and set aside. Mix the lemon juice and salt in a large bowl. Then cut the apples horizontally into slices ⅛" to ¼" thick. (Note: do not core the apples before slicing.) Put the large center slices into the lemon and salt mixture. (Save the small end pieces for apple sauce.) Soak slices in mixture for three minutes and then remove and pat dry with paper towels. Place apple slices on a wire rack on top of a cookie sheet and put in oven set at 140°. Leave the oven door slightly ajar during the drying process. Let apples dry until they are leathery in texture (approximately 4 to 5 hours).

When the apples are dry, remove them from the oven and allow them to cool completely. While waiting, cut off the curved head of the wire hanger and bend the remaining wire into a circle approximately 10" in diameter (cut off excess wire). Thread the apple slices onto the wire circle by poking one end of wire through the core in each slice. Carefully pull the slices within 2" of the opposite end. Continue to thread apple slices until all but 2" on each end of the wire is covered. Twist the ends of the wire together. Attach a ribbon bow at the twisted end, and glue baby's breath, cinnamon sticks, or small bunches of wheat to the wreath if you wish. You might like to make mini-wreaths with the leftover dried apple chunks.

Make an apple puzzle . . . with an apple!

You will need: apples (one for each child)
                  sharp paring knife

When your kids ask for apples, serve them in this clever way—you're sure to get a "puzzled" look on their faces when you hand them the fruit!

Wash apples. Then, with a sharp, pointed knife, cut each apple around its circumference in zig-zag fashion. The point of the knife should reach all the way to the core. When you have cut all the way around the apple, take it apart. Give the cut-up apples to your kids and ask them to put them back together again. Young children, particularly, love this simple game, and they will think you are quite clever to have figured it out!

Start a costume trunk

You will need: a large box or trunk
old clothing such as hats, dresses, scarves, shoes, shirts, purses, etc.

Children love dressing up and pretending they are Mom, Dad, or a host of imaginative characters. Stimulate their play by putting together a costume trunk. It will also come in handy for last-minute costumes for trick or treating, if your family celebrates Halloween.

Start your collection with old dresses and suits. If you don't have a used bridesmaid's dress or Hawaiian shirt hanging in the back of your closet, look for them at garage and estate sales. You'll probably find some funny hats, costume jewelry, and elbow-length gloves along the way!

Here are some basic items to get you and your kids started: large scarves; party and professional hats (firefighter, baseball player, nurse, etc.); costume jewelry; dresses, shirts, nightgowns, vests; wigs; boots, slippers, shoes; purses, backpacks, small suitcases; large piece of cloth for capes, shawls and stage curtains; face paints (see Activity 42).

Once your costume trunk is full of props and disguises, you'll find it invaluable for entertaining young children on a rainy or cold day and ideal for costuming kids for amateur productions and masquerade parties.

Homemade face paint

You will need: 1 teaspoon corn starch
½ teaspoon water
½ teaspoon cold cream
food coloring (variety of colors)
small yogurt container, clean and dry (one for each color paint)
small paintbrush

Face painting done in creative shapes and designs is a nice alternative to wearing a mask on Halloween night (masks can be very frightening to preschoolers and they obscure vision when a child is walking up and down steps or when crossing the street). In addition to using face paint to complete a Halloween costume, kids will enjoy this recipe for birthday parties, staging a backyard play and for dress-up on a rainy day.

The process of making homemade face paint will give a school-age child a valuable experience in following directions, measuring ingredients, and combining and experimenting with colors.

Stir together the corn starch and cold cream until well-blended. Add water and stir. Add food coloring, one drop at a time until you get the desired color. Experiment with the colors by adding more drops of the same color for a darker paint or by adding a different color to create a new shade. Three drops of blue and one drop of green food color will create turquoise. Two drops of yellow and one drop of red blends into orange. Two drops of blue and one drop of red will make violet. Paint designs on faces with a small paintbrush; remove with soap and water. The face paint may be stored in covered yogurt containers.

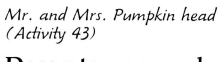

*Mr. and Mrs. Pumpkin head
(Activity 43)*

Decorate uncarved pumpkins and gourds

You will need: pumpkin or gourd (one for
each person)
permanent, felt-tipped
marking pens
acrylic paints, paintbrushes
glue
straight pins
newspaper
"found" items (see below)

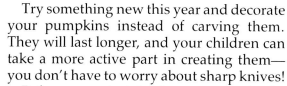

Try something new this year and decorate your pumpkins instead of carving them. They will last longer, and your children can take a more active part in creating them—you don't have to worry about sharp knives!

Before you start to decorate, wash the pumpkins or gourds and dry them thoroughly with a towel. Then let the children scout out the house for "found" items they can use in decorating: buttons, string, ribbon and bows, construction paper, shiny paper, stickers, hats, cotton balls, candy, sunglasses, doll accessories, dried weeds and flowers, pins and medals, cardboard tubes, fabric scraps.

Place all the items collected on a newspaper-covered work surface. Give each child a pumpkin or gourd and let each draw features on it with felt-tipped markers, or paint them on with acrylic paint. Once the features are done, the real fun begins. Add hair, beards, accessories, etc., by gluing items to the pumpkins or attaching them with straight pins.

Display the pumpkins or gourds around the house, on your porch, along a walkway, or perched on a tree branch, ready to catch the attention of October guests.

More blessed to give . . . (Activity 44)

Ways to share at Thanksgiving

You will need: a family commitment to share

By the time Thanksgiving vacation arrives, children are already talking about what they want for Christmas. Promotions, enticing ads, and conversations with friends begin to focus on "things" and the illusion of "having to have" coveted items. What a timely holiday Thanksgiving can be! When celebrated in its true meaning, Thanksgiving can change our focus. Taking time to thank God for what we already have and sharing our wealth with others can put us back on track in a hurry.

Thanksgiving is an ideal time to think about how you and your children can give to your community. Call a family meeting, and decide together what you would like to do. Your project may continue into December and culminate with Christmas. Whatever the project, everyone—kids and grown-ups alike—will benefit from the experience. And the "giving spirit" that is fostered in the children may last a lifetime!

Consider trying one of these projects:
- Collect food in your neighborhood and donate it to a local food shelf.
- Bake cookies or prepare a meal and deliver it to someone you know who is homebound.
- Sort through your closets and drawers for usable clothing that can be given to local relief agencies.
- Invite a visiting foreign student to your Thanksgiving Day celebration.

Mini pumpkin weed doll

You will need: 1 miniature pumpkin
2 quarter-inch dowels or sticks, 10" long
string or raffia
dried weeds
masking tape
4" length of lightweight wire
a piece of soft bark or dried corn husk
straw flowers (optional)

Collect a bag full of dried weeds from along a roadside, in a field, or even between the cracks of concrete in a parking lot or alley. Use a miniature pumpkin for the head and the weeds for a body, and you can create a clever fall decoration for your home or yard.

Poke one dowel into the bottom of the pumpkin, pushing it in until it is secure. Lay the second dowel across the first 1" below the pumpkin. Tape the dowels together tightly. This forms the frame for the doll. Attach weeds crosswise and lengthwise to cover the doll frame, tying the weeds to the frame with string or raffia where the dowels intersect. (You may wish to secure the weeds on the arms also.) Add straw flowers for color, if you wish. Wind a piece of bark or corn husk around the weeds just under the pumpkin to serve as a bodice. Add a few straw flowers for a mini corsage.

TIE

Form a loop with the wire and wind around the doll just under the base of the pumpkin head for a hanger.

WRAP CORNHUSK HERE

Thanks to all (Activity 46)

Pilgrim ship table favors from walnut shells

You will need: walnuts in the shell
(enough for each guest to
have a half)
nutcracker
toothpicks
glue
white construction paper
white typing paper, cut into
2" x 2" squares
pen or pencil
scissors

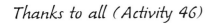

Let the children help prepare for your Thanksgiving meal by making table favors from walnut shells.

Show the children how to crack the walnuts so that they get two halves. Pick out the nuts and set them aside. (Use the nuts in a special holiday salad or add to the turkey stuffing.)

Cut the construction paper into small triangular pieces (1½" x 1½") and write the name of a guest or family member on each. Then thread a toothpick through each triangle "sail." Poke the toothpick into the center of a walnut shell half. If the toothpick won't stand firmly in place, add a drop of glue. Make a boat for each person who will be dining with you. Place them beside the appropriate plates at your table.

As the guests arrive, give each person several small paper squares. Ask everyone to write short Thanksgiving statements showing appreciation for people present at the gathering ("I am thankful that Uncle Bob is so funny," etc.). Roll the papers into tight scrolls and place them in the appropriate boats. As the meal begins, have everyone at the table share the messages in their boats.

Serving bowl sculpture with mini pumpkins

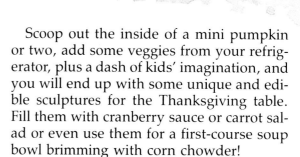

You will need: miniature pumpkins (one for each child)

knife and spoon (for carving out pumpkins)

vegetables such as celery (with leafy tops), radishes, carrots, green beans, cherry tomatoes, artichoke leaves, etc.

raisins and other dried fruits

miniature marshmallows and almonds

toothpicks

serving plates (one for each person)

Scoop out the inside of a mini pumpkin or two, add some veggies from your refrigerator, plus a dash of kids' imagination, and you will end up with some unique and edible sculptures for the Thanksgiving table. Fill them with cranberry sauce or carrot salad or even use them for a first-course soup bowl brimming with corn chowder!

Carefully cut off the top of each pumpkin and clean out the seeds (as you would when carving a Jack-o-Lantern). Place each pumpkin on a serving plate. If it doesn't sit completely upright, trim the bottom of the pumpkin so that it sits flat. Let the children create their own sculptures by attaching raw vegetables, raisins, nuts, etc., to the pumpkins with toothpicks. They may wish to try making a turkey, a ship, or a pilgrim.

Use the sculptures the same day they are created to maximize freshness—the vegetables tend to wilt quickly.

Leave it 'til last (Activity 48)

Make chocolate leaves to garnish your holiday dessert

You will need: fresh rose, camellia, mint,
  or gardenia leaves
4 oz. semi-sweet chocolate
  chips
custard dish
waxed paper
cookie sheet
double boiler or microwave
raspberries, orange rind,
  cherries (optional)

Kids will have fun licking the chocolate off their sticky fingers when they're done, and guests will marvel at the elegant dessert placed before them!

Wash leaves and dry them thoroughly. Melt chocolate chips in the microwave (about 2-3 minutes at high setting), stirring twice, or melt on top of the stove in a double-boiler. Let the melted chocolate cool slightly until it is comfortable to the touch. Place waxed paper on cookie sheet.

Dip the veined side of each leaf into the chocolate, using the stem as a handle. Be careful not to get the chocolate on the other side of the leaf. When the veined side is completely covered with chocolate, lay it on the waxed paper, chocolate side up. Continue process for each leaf. Place leaves in the refrigerator for 15-30 minutes, until the chocolate is firm. Remove from refrigerator. Starting at the stem end, slowly and carefully peel the leaves off the chocolate. Arrange the chocolate leaves in clusters on your pie, cake, sherbet, or ice cream. You might add raspberries, orange rind, or cherries to complete the garnish.

Chocolate leaves can also be stored in the freezer for future use.

"Pass" the cookies (Activity 49)

Bake football cookies

You will need: 1 empty two-pound coffee can for large cookies or empty tomato sauce can for small cookies

1 package of your favorite chocolate refrigerator cookie dough (or mix a batch of your favorite homemade dough)

rolling pin

cookie sheets

canned white butter frosting (or mix your own)

1 zip-lock style plastic bag

Celebrate the end of the football season or the Super Bowl with homemade football cookies. You start by making your own cookie cutter!

Wash and dry the can, and cut off the bottom. Then bend the rim until it is in the shape of a football. Roll out the cookie dough and cut cookie shapes with the can cutter. Place cookies on cookie sheets and bake according to the package or recipe instructions. To frost cooled cookies, spoon frosting into the plastic bag. Cut a small hole in one bottom corner. Squeeze the frosting through the hole, making stitching marks and laces on the cookies as illustrated.

GO TEAM!

BENT CAN
COOKIE CUTTER

Activities for Winter

Regardless of whether you live in the cold North or in the warm sunbelt, winter means shorter days and longer nights. It is a time for drawing in, and if we dare take a cue from nature, we might allow ourselves to hibernate a bit. Schedules already crammed with commitments to jobs, organizations, school, and church are stretched to the limit as the holidays approach. Everyone shifts into overdrive, and often the family's emotional climate suffers, for there seems to be little time for one another.

A five-year-old boy I know left this message for his mother who was caught up in the rush: "MOM—PLEASE DON'T SNARL IN DECEMBER." Do you "snarl" in December? Do you resent the pressures that the winter months bring? Perhaps we should all pay attention to our kids a little more. Children invite us to share with them and enjoy the season in meaningful ways: making a snowman, preparing homemade gifts for family and friends, assembling a big jigsaw puzzle, reading a story together. In spending time with our kids we are given the opportunity to savor what is precious to us, and we're put back on the right track.

This section is filled with activities for Christmas, Hanukkah, New Years, Valentine's Day, and all the days in between. There are ideas for making gifts for teachers and friends and neighbors, clever decorations for the outside and inside of your home, a gingerbread village just right for kids to make with cousins or friends, and a host of other holiday projects. Also included are ideas for a special family New Year's party, complete with games, munchies, and lots of reminiscing. And if you're tired of the same old valentines, check out some of the unique ones here!

This winter, when things appear to be getting out of hand, pause for a moment now and then to look at yourself in the light of the true direction you wish to take—as an individual, a parent, and a family. Give your child a hug, share a treat, and *relax!* We can't do everything— so let's concentrate on what's important.

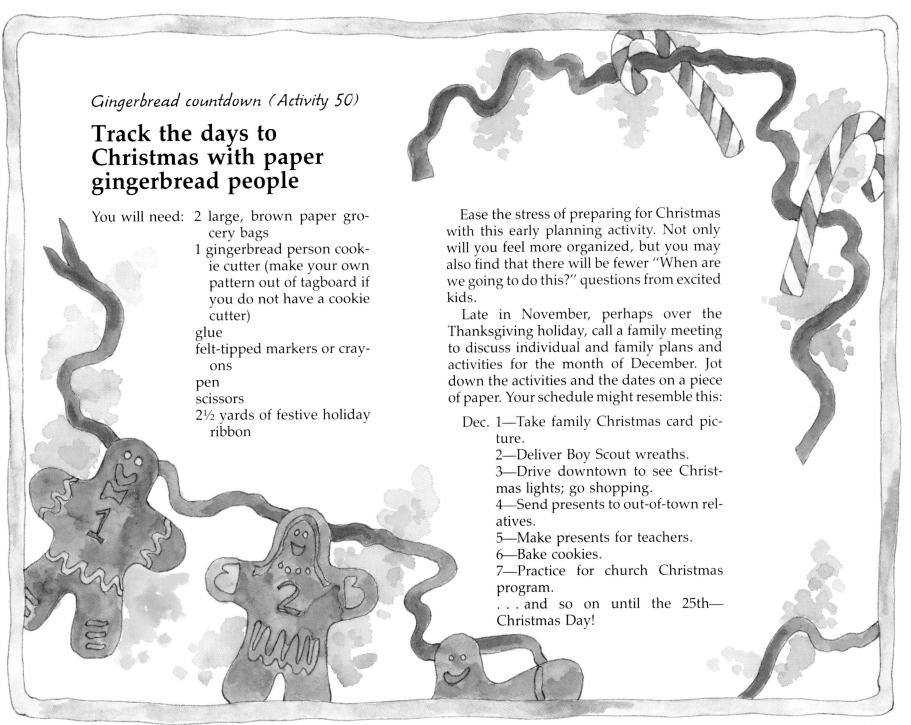

Gingerbread countdown (Activity 50)

Track the days to Christmas with paper gingerbread people

You will need: 2 large, brown paper grocery bags
1 gingerbread person cookie cutter (make your own pattern out of tagboard if you do not have a cookie cutter)
glue
felt-tipped markers or crayons
pen
scissors
2½ yards of festive holiday ribbon

Ease the stress of preparing for Christmas with this early planning activity. Not only will you feel more organized, but you may also find that there will be fewer "When are we going to do this?" questions from excited kids.

Late in November, perhaps over the Thanksgiving holiday, call a family meeting to discuss individual and family plans and activities for the month of December. Jot down the activities and the dates on a piece of paper. Your schedule might resemble this:

Dec. 1—Take family Christmas card picture.
2—Deliver Boy Scout wreaths.
3—Drive downtown to see Christmas lights; go shopping.
4—Send presents to out-of-town relatives.
5—Make presents for teachers.
6—Bake cookies.
7—Practice for church Christmas program.
. . . and so on until the 25th—Christmas Day!

To make the countdown line, cut apart the brown bags to make two large pieces of paper. Fold each piece across the top, forming a double layer large enough to fit your cookie cutter. Place the cookie cutter on the paper with the top of its head on the fold. Trace around the cookie cutter. Continue until you have made 25 figures. Cut out the figures, being careful not to cut through the fold. Let the children color features on the shapes. Number the figures from 1 to 25. Then open up the figures and print on the inside the activity that corresponds with the day on the front. Lay the ribbon on your work surface and slip each figure over the ribbon, beginning with figure 1. Glue the backside of the ribbon to the figures to keep them in place. Then put a dot of glue on the inside bottom of each figure and pinch it shut. Hang the countdown line across your mantel or a large window or along a wall. Each morning until Christmas, let the children open the gingerbread person for the day to remind everyone of the activity inside! (Adults may wish to keep track of all the activities on a personal calendar.)

FOLD

GLUE

ADD DROPS OF GLUE TO CLOSE FIGURE

Make popcorn garlands for tree

Bake Cookies

13

Print a family holiday card/letter

You will need: 1 snapshot of each member of the family doing something he or she has enjoyed during the past year, such as carving a pumpkin, ice skating for the first time, playing baseball, making a sand castle, etc.
1 piece of 9″ x 12″ white construction paper
tape
black pen or typewriter

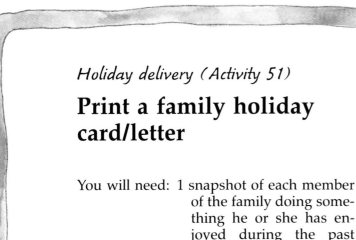

Tape the pictures to the construction paper in whatever arrangement you choose. If you wish, cut out the figures in the snapshots, trimming away backgrounds. Leave enough space under or alongside each picture for a short paragraph. Type or write a paragraph to accompany each picture. Include the names and ages of each child and a quote by each child that describes the activities he or she has enjoyed during the past year, especially the one pictured. Then, in the center of the page or at the bottom, add your own comments and extend holiday wishes from the whole family. Allow the children to sign their names and add their own artistic touches.

Take the completed project to a print shop. Upon request, many print shops will have your letter printed the same day. Prices vary according to the paper you choose and the quantity you order.

Door-to-door (Activity 52)

Decorate kids' doors

You will need: large piece of butcher or art paper the size of your kid's bedroom door(s). (Piece small sheets together if necessary.)
construction paper, fabric scraps, glitter, novelty tems, string
paints, felt-tipped markers
glue or tape
scissors
notepad and pencil

Here's a fun way to give kids free reign to their artistic impulses while adding a holiday touch to your home. With a door-size piece of paper and a few art supplies, your kids will keep busy an entire afternoon completing this project.

Lay paper flat on a work surface. If your children share a room you may divide the paper into parts with a pencil line so each child has a "space," or the kids may wish to work together on a design. Use construction paper, glitter, paints, and other available materials to make a colorful holiday picture. For extra fun, add a "mailbox" to the lower portion of the paper by attaching a large envelope and a notepad with a pencil hanging on a string. Throughout the holiday season, family members and guests may write greetings to the child. Kids always love to get notes, especially those that praise them for accomplishments, compliment them for their kindness to others, and communicate to them how much they are loved.

When the project is finished and dry, hang the decorated paper on the bedroom door with masking tape or small nails. You might string minilights around the doorway to draw attention to the holiday door.

Homemade gift wrap

You will need: brown paper bags, butcher or shelf paper, or any large piece of paper
alphabet rubber stamps (available from toy stores)
ink pad (can be purchased in colors of red and green)

Kids will enjoy keeping busy on a cold December afternoon printing up their own gift wrap. Homemade gift wrap made from butcher or shelf paper and brown paper bags is economical and it adds a personalized and charming touch to the gift you are giving.

Cut paper bags open if you are using them. Lay paper out on work surface. Press stamps on the ink pad and print the paper. Preschool children may enjoy stamping out the ABCs in a pattern around the paper. School-age children can become acquainted with other cultures by printing Merry Christmas in different languages, for example: "Joyeux Noel" (French), "Feliz Navidad" (Spanish), "God Jul" (Swedish), "Fröhliche Weihnachten!" (German).

Just for you (Activity 54)

Personalized gift wraps

You will need: items unique to the person
receiving the gift.

Ask your kids what trait they think of
when they reflect on a certain friend or family member and you'll have the beginnings
of a gift wrap idea! Here are some examples
just to get you started:

If the person loves shopping, wrap the
gift with a map of your local shopping mall.
Instead of a ribbon, use a long cash register
receipt or tape several together!

For a sports enthusiast, wrap the gift with
a page from a sports magazine and tie it up
with a new headband or a pair of sweat
socks.

If the recipient enjoys gardening, wrap
the gift with a floral design fabric and top
it with bunches of seed packets tied together
for a clever bow.

Wrap a gift for someone with a great sense
of humor in the comic section from the Sunday newspaper. Write your own joke in the
gift enclosure.

For the person who loves to cook, print a
special recipe on the wrapping paper. Fill
the package with the ingredients called for
in the recipe. Attach a kitchen utensil or
gadget to the bow.

Map it out (Activity 55)

Locate holiday card origins on a map

You will need: map of the United States, North America, or the world
scissors
tape or thumb tacks
envelopes from incoming holiday greetings

Whether you and your kids are brushing up on your geography or learning the locations of states, capitals, and countries for the first time, this activity will be educational and fun to do each day throughout the month of December.

Post the map where it is seen readily. Then, as holiday greetings arrive in your mailbox each day, share the messages with your kids and save the envelopes the cards come in. Cut off the postmark from each envelope. Read the location printed on the postmark, locate it on your map, and tack or tape the postmark to the correct spot. If the location happens to be a small town that is not printed on the map, use the closest major city as a reference point.

In addition, older children may enjoy calculating the distance the card traveled to get to your home. And save the postage stamps—your kids can start a new hobby that can last a lifetime.

To and from (Activity 56)

Holiday gift tags

You will need: several pieces of 4" x 6" plain notepaper or construction paper (depending on the number of tags you make)

pen

X-acto knife

2" x 3" piece of heavy mylar or acetate (available from art or office supply stores)

acrylic stenciling paint (variety of colors)

sponge

spring-type clothespins (one for each color paint)

paper plate, newspaper

paper punch, scissors

twine or ribbon

double-sided tape

CHILD'S DRAWING

MYLAR STENCIL

Here's a way to make a gift tag an original creation from start to finish. Stencil dozens of them, hang them on a metal loop, and they'll be ready to use all through the holidays.

Fold the notepaper pieces in half to form little cards. Then let your child draw a simple holiday picture on the front of one piece of folded paper: Christmas tree, star, poinsettia, gifts, snowflakes, etc. Emphasize that the picture should be kept simple—the more basic the drawing, the easier it will be to transfer onto the mylar or acetate. Once the picture is finished, an adult or older child can trace the drawing onto the mylar or acetate. Then, place the mylar or acetate on cardboard and carefully cut around the outline of the drawing with the X-acto knife. (Note: an adult should complete this step.) Discard the cut-out piece. You now have a stencil. Back the stencil with two pieces of double-sided tape and attach it to a piece of folded notepaper.

STENCIL LIGHTLY TAPED
TO NOTEPAPER

Cut the sponge into pieces approximately 2″ x ½″ x 2″, and clip the pieces to the clothespins. You should have one for each color paint. Pour a small amount of paint onto the paper plate, and, using the clothespin as a handle, dip the sponge into the paint. Blot several times on newspaper, then lightly dab the sponge on the stencil figure. The paint will dry almost immediately because of the light application. Gently lift the stencil off the notepaper. Repeat for remaining tags.

When tags are completely dry, punch holes in the top left-hand corner, attach ribbons, and write messages on the inside.

You may also make "all occasion" gift tags for use year-round. Store them with your gift wrapping materials. A gift tag stamped with your kids' creativity will probably be appreciated as much as the gift itself.

Over the river and through the crumbs (Activity 57)

Build a graham cracker village

You will need: 1 box of graham crackers (some for building and some for munching!)
gumdrops, Lifesavers, chocolate chips, licorice strings, cake decorating sprinkles, raisins, almonds, coconut, Shredded Wheat cereal, cinnamon sticks, cotton balls, and other items for decorating houses
sharp knife
table knife or small spatula
small mixing bowl and mixer
bread board or large tray
empty individual milk cartons or half-pint cream cartons
3 egg whites
1 teaspoon cream of tartar
1 lb. powdered (confectioners) sugar, sifted
twigs, clay, white confetti, artificial snow (optional)

Skip the trouble of baking gingerbread, and make these miniature gingerbread houses in a jiffy—with graham crackers! Arrange the completed houses with twig-trees and bushes and miniature toy people and you'll have an enchanting village for the family to play with and enjoy.

To make the icing that holds the houses together: Combine 3 egg whites and 1 teaspoon cream of tartar in a small mixing bowl. Beat until stiff peaks form. Add 1 lb. powdered sugar and continue beating until the mixture is thick and holds its shape. Cover the icing with a damp cloth when not using it.

Begin construction of a basic house by cementing graham crackers to the sides of an individual milk carton with icing. (Older children may wish to try building a house without the carton frame.) Allow sides to dry partially before adding the roof. An adult can cut additional graham cracker pieces into interesting shapes with a sharp knife. These pieces can be used to create different sorts of buildings: barns, woodsheds, outhouses, stores, churches, etc.

Once the basic buildings are dry, decorate them with gumdrops, candies, chocolate chips, raisins, and other items you have collected. Dot some icing along the edges of roofs and attach gumdrops for colorful borders, or pile Lifesavers on top of a roof to make a chimney. Stuff the chimney with cotton to give the illusion of smoke. Spread some icing on top of the roofs to resemble snow. Create thatched roofs by cementing Shredded Wheat cereal on top of the houses. Let your imagination run wild.

When all the buildings are complete, arrange them on a bread board or large tray. Tie together sticks for trees and cinnamon sticks for wood piles and anchor them in small balls of clay or icing. Sprinkle coconut around for a winter scene (you may use white confetti or artificial snow). Wind white minilights around the village to create an enchanting effect.

Christmas tree ornaments

These homemade creations add a personal touch to the family tree, and they also make unique gifts for teachers, neighbors, and friends. People of all ages can enjoy an afternoon or evening of making ornaments together. Just be sure to plan ahead so you have all the basic supplies.

Fresh cranberry and marshmallow wreath ornament

You will need: fresh cranberries
                miniature marshmallows
                thin florist wire
                holiday ribbon
                pieces of orange rind (optional)

Young children who enjoy threading buttons and beads will be adept at making this ornament. It makes a colorful addition to the tree, and when the holidays are over, you can hang it outside on a tree branch for a treat for the birds!

Cut the wire into 16″ lengths. Begin by threading a cranberry on the wire, leaving about 1½″ of wire at the end. Alternate cranberries, marshmallows, and orange rind (optional). When the wire is almost covered, twist it into a wreath shape. Twist end pieces of wire together. Attach a ribbon to the wire and hang it on the tree.

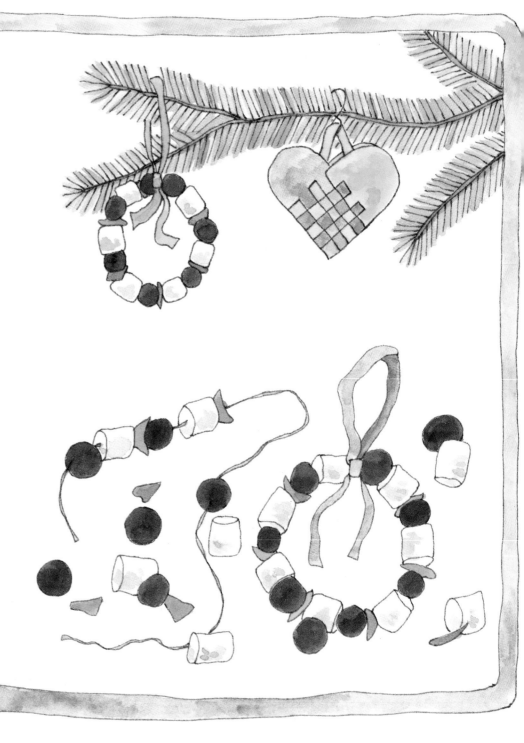

Woven holiday hearts

You will need: 2 sheets of foil art paper or construction paper or felt (in two different colors)
scissors (one pair for each person, if possible)
special treats to fill finished baskets (optional)

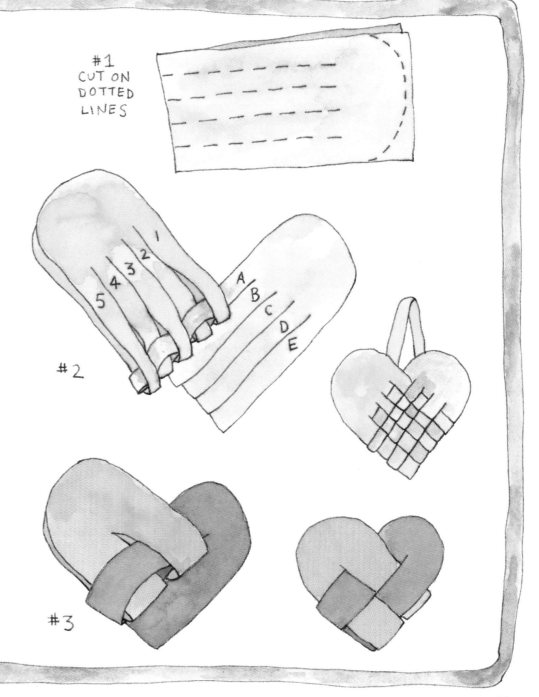

These Scandinavian basketlike ornaments can be filled with candies, peanuts, raisins, or even a heart-shaped cookie.

Cut the paper or felt into 7" x 2" strips. Fold each strip in half lengthwise as illustrated in diagram 1 and round the ends and cut slits as indicated. Begin weaving by taking strip A and placing it through strip 1. Continue to weave A in and out all the strips. Weave B, C, D, and E in the same manner. (See diagram 2.) To make a handle, cut a 7" x ½" strip of paper or felt. Glue or staple the strip to the top center pieces of the heart.

Note: Beginners may wish to make the heart as illustrated in diagram 3, using only two wide strips.

These baskets may also be used at Easter or on May Day. If you wish, simply enlarge the pattern.

#1
CUT ON
DOTTED
LINES

#2

#3

Edible light catchers (Activity 59)

Make stained-glass Hanukkah cookies

You will need: ½ cup soft margarine
¾ cup packed brown sugar
⅓ cup honey
1 egg
1 teaspoon vanilla
½ teaspoon baking soda
½ teaspoon salt
2½-3 cups unsifted flour
¾ lb. bag assorted colored
hard candies
2 foil-lined cookie sheets
clear plastic bags
hammer or mallet
wooden cutting board
2 mixing bowls
1 small bowl for each color
of candy
string, yarn, or ribbon

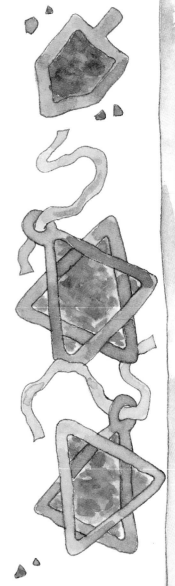

Include friends and family in an afternoon of creative cookie baking to celebrate Hanukkah, the Jewish festival of lights. All ages will enjoy this project!

Step 1: Blend together margarine, brown sugar, honey, and vanilla. In a separate bowl, combine baking soda, salt, and flour. Add dry ingredients to sugar mixture and stir until dough is smooth. If dough is too dry, add water, a tablespoon at a time; if too sticky, add flour. Cover and chill for one hour.

Step 2: Let children unwrap candies and sort by color. (Great for helping young children learn colors!) Place each sorted pile into a plastic bag and fasten shut. Place bags on cutting board and carefully crush candy with a hammer or mallet. Empty bags into individual bowls, keeping colors separate.

Step 3: Preheat oven to 350°. Flour hands and cutting board, then roll dough into ¼" thick "snakes." For each cookie, pinch dough together on foil-lined cookie sheet to form Hanukkah symbols like a menorah or dreidle. Add a loop of dough at the top, if you plan to hang it in a window.

Sprinkle crushed candy evenly into the sections of the cookies. Bake 6-8 minutes or until cookies are lightly brown and candy is melted. Let them cool completely before carefully removing them from the foil. String ribbon or yarn through the loop and the cookie is ready to hang in your window or be given as a special Hanukkah gift! (Note: the recipe will make approximately 18-24 cookies 3" in diameter.)

Crystal clear (Activity 60)

Winter ice candles

You will need: (for small candles) medium size balloon, empty plastic margarine tub, votive candle, food coloring (optional)

(for large candles) empty, one-gallon plastic ice cream bucket, vegetable oil, votive candle

This activity is suited for colder, northern climates, where snow and ice are usual winter fare. Creating lights in ice is easy and fun to do, and the flickering lights add a warm glow to a cold night.

Small ice candles

Fill the balloon with water until it is about the size of a softball, and add a drop of food coloring if you wish. Blow once into the balloon and then tie a knot in it. Place the balloon in the margarine tub and set outside in freezing temperature. If it is not cold enough to freeze outside, place it in your freezer. After 4-5 hours a fairly thick shell of ice should form inside the balloon. Check by shaking the balloon gently; if the outside is hard and water can be heard sloshing around inside, it is time to pop the balloon. Discard balloon. Pour excess water out to form a cavity in the middle. This is where the candle will be placed. Freeze candle holder for two hours, until it is very hard. At sunset, place votive candle in center of ice candle holder and light it. Place candle outside by your door to welcome visitors. Note: If the temperature is above freezing the next day, bring the candle holder inside and store in your freezer.

Large ice candles

Rub a thin coating of vegetable oil on the inside of the ice cream pail. Fill pail with water and place outside in freezing temperature. If it is not cold enough to freeze outside, place pail in your freezer. When the water is partially frozen (4-5 hours), scoop out a cavity in the middle and insert a votive candle. When the ice is frozen solid, remove it from the ice cream pail. At sunset, light the candle and place by your door. To store the candle, leave outside if temperatures are below freezing, or bring in and put in your freezer.

USE FAUCET TO FILL BALLOON ↙

ICE SHELL ↑

SCOOPED OUT CAVITY FOR CANDLE ↙

Give it a glow (Activity 61)

Snowball lamp

You will need: 40-50 firm snowballs
votive or pillar candle

This is a favorite activity for young children!

In your front yard, place 12-14 snowballs together in a ring shape. Place the candle in the middle of the ring. Add a second ring of 10-12 snowballs on top of the first. Continue to pile snowball rings on top, making each ring slightly smaller than the one before until you run out of snowballs. Leave an opening at the top. At sunset, an adult can light the candle.

Light the way (Activity 62)

Punched-tin luminarias

You will need: plain tin can with all rough
edges pinched flat and
smooth
hammer
bath towel
votive candle
nail
permanent black felt-tipped
marker
holiday ribbon (optional)

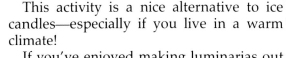

This activity is a nice alternative to ice candles—especially if you live in a warm climate!

If you've enjoyed making luminarias out of paper bags and sand, you'll have fun making this version with tin cans and a hammer. School-age kids can create their own designs, adding their special touch to your family's holiday decorations.

Fill the can with water and place in your freezer (or outside, if you live in a cold climate). When the ice is frozen solid, remove from freezer. Using a permanent felt-tipped marker, dot a design on the side of the can. You may wish to draw a Christmas tree, star, bell, or some other holiday symbol. Leave 1″ from the bottom of the can undecorated.

Place the can on its side on the bath towel. Carefully hammer out the design by positioning the nail on each of the dots and hammering it through the tin until it hits the ice. (The ice prevents the nail from bending the tin.) Continue punching holes until you have completed your pattern. Allow the ice to melt. Pour out the water that remains in the can, place it ouside, and set a votive candle in the center. At sunset, an adult can light the candle.

Make holiday baskets to share with others

You will need: inexpensive baskets or wooden mushroom boxes

stencils and acrylic stenciling paints (see Activity 55 for stencil directions)

stenciling brushes or pieces of sponge and spring-type clothespins

pinecones

holiday ribbon, gift tags

items to fill baskets: grapefruit, oranges, apples, pears, kiwi, herb teas, gourmet coffee, shelled nuts, specialty items from your area: dried fruits, cheeses, wild berry jams and jellies, wild rice, etc.

date treats (1 package pitted dates, shelled walnut halves, powdered sugar, plastic sandwich bags or small gift box)

fudge sauce (1 cup chocolate chips, ½ cup butter or margarine, 2 cups powdered sugar, 1 cup evaporated milk, 1 teaspoon vanilla, small empty jam jar, heavy sauce pan, wooden spoon)

Plan a Saturday when the whole family can make some easy holiday goodies and assemble them with other holiday treats in a basket to deliver to a neighbor or relative or friend who may be homebound.

Stencil simple designs on the sides of your baskets, using commercially made stencils or those you have created (see Activity 55 for directions on stenciling). While you are waiting for the paint to dry, your young elves may help make the date treat. Meanwhile, older "stove smart" children or adults can make fudge sauce.

Date treat

Place dates, walnut halves, and powdered sugar in bowls, and arrange them in assembly line fashion on your work surface. For each treat, tuck a walnut half in the seed cavity of a date and roll the date in powdered sugar. Package several together in a small gift box or plastic sandwich bag and tie closed with a pretty ribbon.

Fudge sauce

Melt 1 cup chocolate chips and ½ cup butter or margarine in a heavy saucepan. Add 2 cups powdered sugar and 1 cup evaporated milk. Cook until thick, stirring constantly. Remove from heat. Stir in 1 teaspoon vanilla. Allow sauce to cool slightly and then pour it into clean jam jars. When completely cool, screw on lids. Label the contents and refrigerate.

Assemble your gift items in the decorated and stenciled baskets. Add a ribbon and gift tag to each, tuck in a pinecone or two, and schedule a special holiday delivery. Have fun spreading holiday goodwill!

Recycle your Christmas tree

You will need: Christmas tree stripped of
        its decorations
        popcorn garlands
        cranberry marshmallow
          wreaths (Activity 58)
        pretzels
        old bread
        cookie cutters
        pinecones
        peanut butter
        birdseed
        string

Nothing seems more anticlimatic than post-Christmas cleanup. Add some zip to the chore by getting your kids involved in redecorating the Christmas tree once it has been dragged outside. The decorations are simple ornaments of food that your bird friends will soon discover.

If you have already made cranberry marshmallow wreath decorations (see Activity 58) or garlands of popcorn, you have a head start. Add pretzels to the popcorn garlands, or make a new garland from dried bread pieces that the kids cut into fun shapes with cookie cutters.

Gather all the pinecones that have decorated your home and turn them into a treat for the birds, too. Smear globs of peanut butter on them and roll them in birdseed. Tie some string around the top petals of the cone and hang them on the tree.

Place the tree near your kitchen or family room window so your family can enjoy watching the birds feeding. Remember, once you start feeding the birds you need to keep a continuous supply of food for them throughout the winter months—they'll be depending on you.

See you next year! (Activity 65)

Plan a family New Year's party

You will need: slides, videos, or pictures of family activities from the past year
hot cocoa or hot apple cider
popcorn snack (½ cup melted butter or margarine, ½ cup honey, 3 quarts popped popcorn, 1 cup nuts, cookie sheet, small saucepan)

Instead of going out to celebrate the new year, plan a special stay-at-home party with your family. It's a great way to recall the best of times from the past year and to look forward to the next. The next few activities feature things you may want to do at the party (see Activities 67-69). For starters, make some good snacks such as hot cocoa or hot apple cider and try this popcorn-nut munchie:

Popcorn snack

Combine ½ cup melted butter or margarine and ½ cup honey in a small saucepan; heat until well blended. Add 1 cup chopped nuts. Pour over 3 quarts of popcorn and mix well. Spread popcorn mixture in a thin layer on a cookie sheet and bake in 350° oven for 12 minutes until crisp. Stir often to avoid burning.

At the party, enjoy the treats while you view slides, videos, or photos that you've taken over the past year. This activity is good for reminding kids of the many activities in their lives that make them unique. They'll discover how much they have learned, grown, and changed. If there was a death of a friend or a relative during the year, take time to share memories of that person.

The party is also a great time to reminisce over funny and unforgettable moments. Encourage family members to reenact or retell a humorous situation and share their special memories. Consider trying some or all of the following activities at your party (see Activities 66-69).

Make family puppets and act out the year's best events

You will need: paper lunch bags
felt-tipped markers in a variety of colors
construction paper
scissors
glue
string or yarn
fabric and other sewing scraps

Have each member of the family make a puppet that represents him or her, and then put on a family production. "The Year's Favorite Events."

Place a closed paper bag, bottomside up on your workspace. On the bottom of the bag, draw eyes and a nose. (The mouth will be in the fold of the bag.) Draw on hair or glue string or yarn to the bag to represent hair. Add construction paper clothes or cut some from fabric scraps and glue to the bottom half of the bag. When the puppet is completed, practice using it by slipping your hand into the bag and bringing your fingers over the fold. Move the head section of the puppet up and down to make the puppet look as if it is speaking.

Family members can take turns spontaneously performing for the rest, or groups can act out specific events from the past year. Your kids may provide you with some interesting insights into their perception of activities you experienced together. Encourage creativity and storytelling techniques. Above all, have fun!

Illustrate your New Year's resolutions

You will need: plain drawing paper or white construction paper crayons or felt-tipped markers in a variety of colors

Just like adults, children can look ahead to the new year with special resolutions. Perhaps your child would like to learn how to ride a two-wheel bike, plant a garden, take piano lessons, or join a soccer team at the neighborhood park. New Year's resolutions need not be just changes in behavior or task oriented. However, your child may need encouragement to work on some areas that are particularly challenging, such as including younger siblings in games, making the bed regularly, or putting away clothes. Encourage your kids to illustrate their resolution on a piece of paper. When the drawing is complete, write the resolution at the bottom (adults or older siblings can help the younger ones) and hang the paper on a bulletin board or bedroom wall. The drawings will reinforce the challenges your kids have made for the new year and serve as a personal reminder of their goal.

Add your artwork to the project too! Your kids will be interested in knowing what your resolutions are for the coming year. With some support from one another, the resolutions just may be realized!

91

What's my line? (Activity 68)

Holiday card game

You will need: holiday greeting cards you
have received this year

During the busy days of December, holiday greeting cards are often quickly read
by adults and then tossed into a basket. Now
that the pace has calmed down a bit, take
the opportunity to reread your cards with
this family activity. You'll refresh your kids'
memories of friends and family and have
fun as well.

Sort through your holiday greetings and
choose those that come from relatives and
close friends of the family. Everyone playing
the game should sit down in a circle. Pass
out a card to each person. (Younger non-
readers may sit with an adult or older broth-
er or sister. Or, if you have cards that contain
photos of people they would recognize, they
may be able to play the game unassisted.)

Each person takes turns giving clues
about who sent the card he or she is holding.
The rest of the group tries to guess the iden-
tity of the person or persons. Your clues may
be like this: "This family lives in Colorado.
The father is a doctor and the mother is an
aerobics instructor," or "This person visited
us last summer. He comes from another
country." Continue giving clues until someone guesses correctly. Then move on to the
next person in the circle.

If there is a note written on the card, read
it aloud to the whole group—kids especially
enjoy hearing their names mentioned or
news about cousins and friends who are of
the same age.

Don't forget it! (Activity 69)

Make a memory game

You will need: poster board cut into 1½" x
1½" squares
identical pairs of pictures,
drawings, stickers, cou-
pons, cut-outs from mag-
azines, newspapers, ce-
real boxes and packages,
canceled postage stamps
and school photos
glue

Young children generally do better than adults when they play memory games, games made of pairs of cards that players must match (similar to the game show "Concentration"). Create your own homemade version using special stickers, pictures, and other funny things kids find around the house.

Not only do children feel a tremendous sense of success when they play the game, but they are also delighted when their own picture appears on the table!

To make the cards: Glue each item onto a tagboard square (be sure that there are identical items to make a pair). You may make as many as 20 pairs, although if preschoolers are just learning the game you may wish to start with 10 pairs.

To play the game: Shuffle the cards, and then place all cards face down on a table in even rows of 5 cards each. To begin play, the first player turns over one card. (When playing with preschoolers you may wish to say out loud what the card is, such as "A sticker of a pink dinosaur." This helps to reinforce the image.) The player then turns over a second card. If it doesn't match the first card, the player turns the two cards back over and the next player begins. If a player matches the two cards, those cards are given to the player, and he or she takes another turn. Each player plays until he or she no longer makes a match.

The object of the game is to get the most matches—a feat most often accomplished by a child!

Say something nice (Activity 70)

Send in-house valentines

You will need: 1 empty shoe box
1 small notepad and pencil on a string
festive valentine art supplies: doilies, crepe paper, hearts cut from construction paper, stickers, etc.
scissors
glue
tape

Here's a way to help tame the teasing, name calling, and criticism that so often gets in the way of building good relationships between family members—especially between siblings. Take advantage of Valentine's Day and use the holiday and the week preceding it to mend relationships or simply to enhance them in a positive way.

This activity is a non-threatening vehicle for fostering communication in the family and for sharing some of those feelings that are sometimes hard to express eye-to-eye. You may even start a new tradition in your family with the Valentine box!

Cut a 3″ slot down the middle of the shoe box lid. Have the family decorate the lid and the box with colorful valentine materials. Place the lid on the box and tape the sides together. Tape the small notepad and pencil on a string to the top of the box.

One week before Valentine's Day, place the box on your dining room table. Encourage all family members and friends who stop by to pull a piece of paper off the notepad and jot down a special valentine note to each member of the family. (Older siblings or adults may help the younger ones with the writing, or each person may draw a picture that expresses their feelings.)

On Valentine's Day, gather together for a special meal, then open the box and take turns reading the big stack of notes that have accumulated. Enthusiasm will have been building throughout the week, so expect your kids to be quite excited!

Cookie cutter munchies for Valentine's Day

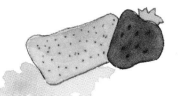

You will need: large and small heart-shaped cookie cutters
(for biscuits) biscuit dough (from your own recipe or a package), bread board, rolling pin, strawberry or raspberry jam
(for sandwiches) whole grain bread, cream cheese, sliced tomatoes, radishes, strawberries
(for afternoon snack) apples, cheese, crackers, cranberry juice and sparkling mineral water

Here are some easy-to-prepare, healthy foods that school-age children can make on their own and proudly serve to hungry family and friends as a special Valentine treat. (Or Moms and Dads can tuck them into unsuspecting lunch boxes!)

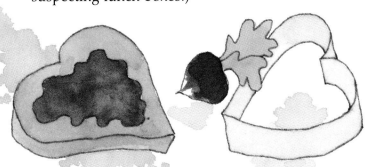

Breakfast biscuits

Follow the directions for preparing your favorite biscuit recipe or use a refrigerated package of biscuits purchased from your supermarket. Roll out the dough on a flour-dusted bread board and cut out heart-shaped biscuits with the cookie cutters. Bake according to directions and serve hot with strawberry or raspberry jam. You might stick the biscuits and jam in a basket and serve as breakfast in bed!

Noon sandwiches

Cut heart shapes from whole grain bread slices, using the larger cookie cutter. Spread cream cheese over each bread slice and top with sliced tomatoes or sliced radishes or sliced strawberries. Arrange on a platter and serve.

Afternoon snack

Cut an apple or two and your favorite cheese into 1/4" slices. Using the small cookie cutter, cut the cheese and apples into heart shapes. Arrange the apple and cheese hearts on a plate and serve with crackers. Mix cranberry juice and sparkling mineral water for a snappy Valentine's Day beverage.

Mend my heart (Activity 72)

Quilted heart valentines

You will need: pieces of quilted material (antique quilted material is especially nice)
plain heavy art paper (available from art supply stores)
glue
scissors
plain paper
straight pins
sewing machine, thread
envelopes
⅛" wide ribbon or heart-shaped buttons (optional)

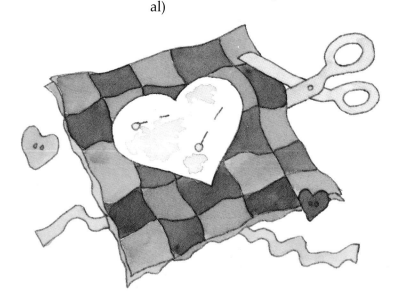

Here's a unique Valentine keepsake that school-age children can make. The activity is especially suited for kids who have been itching to try out your sewing machine.

Cut the quilted fabric into 4" x 4" squares. Cut a 2" x 2" heart-shaped pattern from the plain paper. Cut the art paper into 4" x 8" pieces. (You will need one piece of art paper and one piece of quilted fabric for each Valentine card.)

Pin the heart pattern to a quilted fabric square and cut around the pattern. Remove pins and pattern. Lightly dot heart-shaped quilt piece with glue and attach it to the front side of a piece of artist paper. (This will keep the heart in place as you sew.) Using a zig-zag stitch, sew around the edge of the fabric heart. Fold the paper in half to form a card. Hand sew a ribbon bow or a heart-shaped button to the card for an added touch. These cards are pretty enough to be framed! Or seal them in envelopes for a special Valentine delivery.

Heart-to-heart-to-heart (Activity 73)

Make a cinnamon stick and hearts wall hanging

You will need: 3 medium-sized wooden hearts with hole and wire loop at the top (available from craft and hobby stores)
6 large wooden beads
1 box of cinnamon sticks
2 yards of ¼" wide ribbon
newspaper, red and white acrylic paint, paintbrush or sponge (optional)

If your kids like to thread beads and various shaped objects, they'll enjoy this project. Not only is it easy to make, but the finished product is beautiful! You can hang this "country look" decoration across a window, door, or mantel for Valentine's Day, as well as for the rest of the year.

If you choose to paint the hearts, place them on newspaper and apply red paint with a brush or sponge. Let dry, then paint the other side. When red paint is dry, dot white paint along the edges of the hearts to decorate them.

Tie a knot in the ribbon about 6" from one end. Begin to string the hanging by pulling ribbon through a bead, then a heart, then another bead, then a cinnamon stick. (Take a moment to grate the end of a cinnamon stick to let the kids get a good sniff of fresh cinnamon.) Repeat the sequence until the two remaining hearts are threaded. Finish with a bead, and knot the ribbon. Hang the decoration in your home, or send it as a special valentine to someone you care about.

Create a valentine from Spanish moss and ribbon

You will need: medium-size Styrofoam heart form (available from craft and hobby stores)

1 bag Spanish moss (available from craft and florist shops)

approximately 4 yards each of ⅛″-¼″ wide color co-ordinated ribbon (pink, rose, mauve, cream, white, purple, lavender)

paper cup

glue

paintbrush

baby's breath or small silk flowers (optional)

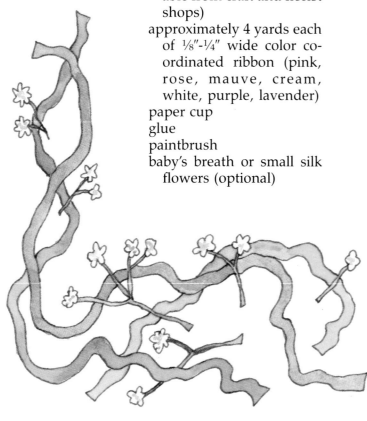

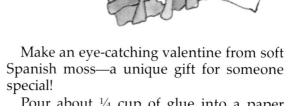

Make an eye-catching valentine from soft Spanish moss—a unique gift for someone special!

Pour about ¼ cup of glue into a paper cup, add a tablespoon of water, and stir until blended. Paint the glue mixture onto the heart form and immediately begin wrapping and sticking the Spanish moss onto the form. Fill in all the empty spaces, adding more glue when necessary. Let dry. When completely dry, wind ribbons around the heart, leaving enough ribbon to tie a bow with streamers. Tuck in baby's breath or small silk flowers, if you wish. Pin a valentine card to a ribbon and present the gift to someone special.

Year-Round Activities

We can celebrate holidays, birthdays, and special occasions with fanfare, joy, and enthusiasm, but what happens with the time in between? A return to routine usually is welcomed after the hectic pace of special events. Children thrive on routines and predictable patterns on which they can rely. Snuggling in bed with a special blanket or stuffed toy while listening to a story told by a caring adult, or saying good-bye to a day with a simple prayer are comforting rituals that bring a sense of continuity to a young life. Rituals on the family level contribute to a secure environment, especially when children are overloaded with stress and feel pressure from uncertainties they cannot control. Family rituals and traditions are important aspects of a healthy homelife.

Much of this book has dealt with ways in which family traditions can be established, centering around the seasons of the year. However, traditions must evolve as a family grows and changes. Some of life's greatest moments occur when we dare to try something new and break the established cycle. That's good to do once in a while, for it teaches our children about flexibility and provides them with opportunities that may develop initiative, creativity, and even an eye for adventure! Supporting and encouraging children in new pursuits shows you value their creativity. You are giving them permission to experiment and grow.

Look for activities in this section that will supplement a topic you are already cultivating with your child, such as reading, music, science, art. The projects can be done year round. For easy access to the basic materials you will use for these projects and others, you might wish to set aside a cupboard, drawer, or box for your supplies. Keep it replenished with the basics: paint, felt-tipped markers, crayons, paintbrushes, pencils, paper, scissors, and glue. A large plastic tablecloth is also nice to have on hand. Use it to cover your work surface, and clean up will be a lot easier. You might also set aside a container for collecting special supplies that will come in handy any time of the year: buttons and beads, sewing scraps, feathers, seashells, cardboard tubes, stickers, string, and clay, to name a few. Then go ahead and have some fun . . . and some prime time together with your kids!

Fly high (Activity 75)

Make a birthday flag

You will need: ½ yard heavy cotton or canvas type fabric
scraps of cotton material for making letters and figures
fabric paint
iron-on appliques (optional)
fusible webbing
½" dowel, 36" long
sewing machine
iron

Fly a personal flag for your child on his or her birthday to emphasize how special the day is and how special the person is!

Cut a 24" x 18" rectangle from the heavy fabric and turn in a ¼" hem on all four sides. Sew down the hem with a zig-zag stitch. Fold ¾" of the left edge to the backside and sew down ½" from the folded edge. Check to see if the dowel fits snugly into the casing that is formed. Take out dowel and sew the casing closed at the top edge only.

Cut out the letters of the child's name from scrap material and, following the manufacturer's instructions, attach the letters to the flag with fusible webbing. If you wish, you may iron on appliques or use iron-on patching material for the letters. Add additional designs to the flag to personalize it, using fabric scraps and paints. For example, if the child was born in Colorado, add a border of mountains, or sew on a baseball and bat if the child plays on a team, or add a bunch of balloons in the child's favorite color. Make the flag special! You may wish to involve the whole family (except the birthday child!) in the process.

When done decorating, slip the dowel into the casing and hang the flag on your porch, from a lamp post or tree, or inside your house. You need not limit the flag's use to birthdays. Fly the flag if your child has had a special day in school or won a big game or comes home with a good report card. You may even want to fly it when things aren't going well, just to show that the family cares and thinks the child is special!

Host a dinosaur party

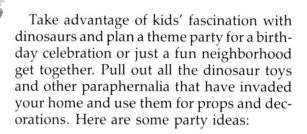

You will need: all the dinosaur paraphernalia hiding in your house (stuffed and plastic toys, posters, books, etc.)

(for cookies) poster board, black felt-tipped marker, scissor, large cookie sheet, rolling pin, sugar cookie dough (from your favorite recipe or from the refrigerated section of your grocery store), paring knife, raisins (optional)

(for fossils) chicken bones from your last chicken dinner, scrub brush, chlorine bleach, dishwashing liquid, white modeling clay, sandbox or foil roasting pan filled with clean sand, strainers, spoons, small shovels, plastic sandwich bags, newspaper and shoe boxes (optional)

(for volcano) sandbox or large, foil roasting pan filled with sand, empty and clean frozen juice container, ¼ cup baking soda, ⅔ cup white vinegar, ⅓ cup dishwashing liquid, red food coloring

Take advantage of kids' fascination with dinosaurs and plan a theme party for a birthday celebration or just a fun neighborhood get together. Pull out all the dinosaur toys and other paraphernalia that have invaded your home and use them for props and decorations. Here are some party ideas:

Bake dinosaur cookies—"Dino-bite!"

Instead of birthday cake, create special dinosaur cookies! Have your child draw his or her favorite dinosaur with a marker on poster board. Cut out the shape and set it aside. Roll the sugar cookie dough onto the cookie sheet. (The cookie will be too large to transfer to the sheet if the dough is rolled out on the counter or on a bread board.) Place the dinosaur cut-out on top of the dough and carefully cut around it with a paring knife. Remove excess dough from around the cookie. Decorate the cookie with raisin eyes, etc., if you wish. Bake according to the recipe instructions, allowing some extra time for the added size of the cookie. When slightly cool, carefully transfer the cookie to a cooling rack. Make enough cookies to go around.

Dig for bones

Save all the chicken bones from your last chicken dinner, remove any meat, and place the bones in a pot of water. Boil the bones until they are clean. To make them white, add some detergent and bleach. When clean, spread them out on a towel to dry.

Before the party, take the clean bones and bury them in your backyard sandbox (or in a large foil roasting pan filled with sand). At the party, have the kids sift through the sand with spoons, strainers, and shovels. Place the bones they find in plastic sandwich bags. When everyone has collected a fair number of "fossils," dust off the bones and go on to the next activity.

Encourage the kids to create their own creatures with the bones they have found. Use white modeling clay to hold the bones together. Have the children name their creatures. Wrap the finished creations in newspaper and place in shoe boxes for safe transport home.

Make your own volcano

As a grand finale to your party, gather the kids around for a safe but impressive mini volcanic eruption!

Ask the kids to make a big mound of sand in the sandbox (or in the foil roaster filled with sand). They may also enjoy placing their tiny dinosaur toys around the volcano and adding a few sticks and twigs here and there to complete the prehistoric scene.

In the middle of the mound, bury all but the top of a clean frozen juice can containing ¼ cup baking soda. In another container mix together 1 cup water with ⅔ cup white vinegar and ⅓ cup dishwashing liquid. You may add several drops of red food coloring for a "special effect."

With all eyes on the mound, pour the solution into the small juice can. The eruption will occur immediately!

Strike up the band (Activity 77)

Set up a gadget band

You will need: a variety of small appliances, tools, and housewares, both electric and manual (hair blower, blender, mixer, egg beater, radio, television set, pots and pans, spoons, etc.)
extra extension cords for electric appliances
roll of freezer paper or butcher paper
2 tubes from rolls of gift wrap or paper towels
masking tape
felt-tipped markers

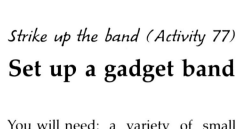

All ages will love this zany representation of a traditional orchestra with unconventional instruments and an unusual musical score. While you're having fun, your kids will be learning that an orchestra is made of sections, musicians read music, and everyday sounds heard around the house can make music!

Gather "instruments" from around the house and assign one to each person. The orchestra works best when there are at least eight members. Decide together how you will group the instruments: radio and television sets in one section, hair dryers in another, etc. The youngest musicians will enjoy banging on pots and pans.

To make your musical score, attach one end of the freezer paper to the cardboard tube, taping it securely. Be sure to have the nonwax surface up—you cannot draw on the waxed side. Then determine a symbol for each section of the orchestra: a sun may represent a hair dryer section, zig-zag lines for televisions and radios, etc. Draw the symbols on the paper in the order you wish to have things played. Continue drawing symbols until you have used up your length of paper, rolling up the paper as you go along. When you are finished, attach the second tube and rewind the paper to the beginning.

Have all the players sit on the floor in their respective sections. The conductor faces the group and holds up the score. Practice playing the instruments by turning appliances on and off or adjusting the volume (TV sets and radios), switching from high to low speed, or banging things together. When everyone is sufficiently warmed up, begin the concert. As the conductor slowly unrolls the score, the instruments are played accordingly. For fun, play the score backwards. You're guaranteed a lot of laughter and some very strange music!

Based on Minneapolis composer/performer Monica Maye's "Home Appliance Orchestra."

Music makers (Activity 78)

Build a milk carton guitar

You will need: a clean, empty half gallon cardboard milk carton with the top taped shut
yardstick
45-50" of nylon fishing line

You can really make music with this simple homemade guitar!

Cut a slit about ½" deep near each end of the yardstick. Cut vertical slits in two sides of the milk carton ⅔ up from the bottom. Insert the yardstick through the carton and position the carton near the center of the yardstick. Make a loop in one end of the fishing line and slip it over the notch on the top of the yardstick. Pull the line over the top of the carton and loop it around the notch at the other end of the yardstick. Tie it securely. Pull the carton to one end of the yardstick.

To play the instrument, strum the string near the bridge (the top edge of the milk carton) with one hand. Pinch the string to the yardstick with the other hand to change pitches. Your kids may soon discover that the numbers printed on the yardstick can be helpful in locating the pitch they need for a song.

Mr. Tambourine Man (Activity 79)

Make a pie plate tambourine

You will need: 1 foil or tin pie plate
6-8 flattened bottle caps
string
ice pick

Here's an old favorite that is easy to make and fun to play when kids want to accentuate the rhythm of the band!

Using the ice pick, an adult should make 6-8 holes around the edge of the pie plate and one hole in each bottle cap. Let the children pull a piece of string through a bottle cap and a hole in the pie plate, making tight knots to hold the bottle cap in place. Be sure to allow enough slack in the string so the cap can move freely and hit the pie plate when it is shaken. Continue this procedure until all caps are attached. Then give it a good shake—you're ready to play!

Blow that tune (Activity 80)

Bottle music

You will need: several empty bottles of exactly the same size (pop bottles, mineral water bottles, or juice bottles work well)
pitcher filled with water

This activity is especially fun to do outside in the summer. You can pour some water out of your bottle to change the pitch and cool yourself off at the same time!

Line up the bottles and pour a different amount of water into each one, starting with a small amount in the first and gradually increasing the amount. Tune the bottles by blowing into them and emptying or adding water to achieve the pitch you desire. Try playing a familiar tune or make up something new. It's even more fun to try duets!

107

Make a personal picture book

You will need: 3 sheets of 8½" x 11" colored construction paper
1 roll of clear adhesive-backed paper
glue
felt-tipped markers in a variety of colors
paper punch
1 yard of ribbon
12 photos of different family members, including one of your child

With relatives often living miles apart, it is hard to maintain close contact with cousins, aunts and uncles, and grandparents. To keep your young child familiar with the faces of important people in his or her life, make a personal picture book. Because the pages will be protected with clear adhesive-backed paper, peanut butter and other sticky stuff can easily be removed with a damp cloth. And when the relatives arrive for the holidays, your child will probably be the first to call them by name even though they have not seen each other in ages.

Cut each sheet of construction paper in half. Glue a photo to the front and back side of each sheet of paper. Under each photo print the name of the person in large letters with markers.

Cut six 8½" x 11" pieces of clear adhesive-backed paper. Cover each sheet of paper, folding the adhesive-backed paper around the right edge of the construction paper to make a durable page. Punch two holes on the left side of each page. Pile the six pages on top of each other with your child's photo on top. Attach the pages together with a piece of string or ribbon tied through the two holes.

Make additional picture books using other topics such as "My neighborhood" (draw or photograph your house, car, park, special tree, neighbors, store, library, etc.).

Tell an original story on cassette and illustrate it

You will need: audiocassette recorder and an audiotape

large sheets of art or construction paper

paints, felt-tipped markers, or crayons

ribbon or yarn

paper punch

Foster your children's interest in books and storytelling by recording their own masterpieces on cassette tape. Even those kids who are too young to read can make their own storybooks!

This activity is often most successful when done on the spur of the moment—when you hear your kids spinning a tale to themselves while playing with their toys, swinging on a park swing, or digging sand at the beach. Listen in and try to remember the story. When you get back home or share a quiet moment, retell the story together. Get out the recorder and encourage the child to tell the story to the machine. Then, as you play back the story, have the child draw illustrations to accompany it. Punch holes in each sheet of paper and tie them together with ribbon in story order to form a book. Replay the story again, this time turning the pages of the book and looking at the pictures.

Designer letters (Activity 83)

Alphabet drawings

You will need: 26 pieces of poster board, 12″ x 12″ (one for each letter of the alphabet)

assorted items whose names start with the sound of each letter of the alphabet (see directions below)

felt-tipped markers
scissors
glue
tempera paints
construction paper

Have fun with your preschooler or kindergartner while reinforcing alphabet skills with this hands-on activity. Once you have created these clever alphabet letters, you can save them to use over and over.

Draw large block letters for each letter of the alphabet on the poster board pieces. Cut them out. If you wish, you may start with just a few letters, such as the first letter of the child's name.

As you begin the project with the first letter you have cut out, tell your child that you are going to look for things that begin with the sound of that letter. For example, the sound "NNNN" in *noodles* is the letter N. Here are some ideas to get you started:

A—apple stamping: Cut an apple into thirds, dip into white tempera paint, and stamp all over a red letter A.

B—buttons and beads: Glue buttons and beads on a black letter B.

C—cereal: Glue bits of your favorite cereal on a white letter C.

D—dots: Use a cotton swab to glue paper punch dots on the letter D.

E—eggshells: Glue crushed eggshells on a white letter E. When dry, paint the eggshells with water colors.

F—fabric: Cover the letter F with flowered fabric scraps.

G—glitter: Glue glitter to a green letter G.

H—hands: Make handprints with tempera paint on the letter H.

I—ice cream. Cut a cone and circles of ice cream from construction paper and glue to the letter I.

J—joints. Cut the letter J into several pieces. Reattach the pieces with brass paper fasteners to make flexible joints.

K—kisses: Apply a heavy coat of lipstick to your child's lips and let him or her smother the letter K with kisses. (Cover the letter with clear, adhesive-backed paper to prevent the lipstick from smearing.)

L—leaves: Glue a colorful assortment of fall leaves to the letter L.

M—money: Glue play money onto the letter M.

N—noodles. Glue macaroni noodles to the letter N.

O—oats. Glue raw (uncooked) oatmeal to the letter O.

P—popcorn: Glue popcorn kernels to a purple letter P.

Q—quail: Cover the letter Q with feathers. Use construction paper to add a beak, eye, and feet.

R—rocks: Glue small rocks to a red letter R.

S—stamps: Glue used postage stamps or promotional stamps from book, record, or magazine clubs on a letter S.

T—tape: Transform the letter T with a variety of masking, electrical, and bandage wrapping tape. Twist and tangle the tape into interesting shapes.

U—ukulele: Glue the letter U to the center of a ukulele cut from brown poster board.

V—valentine: Glue red construction paper hearts to a pink letter V, and decorate with lace and stickers.

W—wood: Glue wood chips to a white W.

X—xylophone: Glue a variety of colored strips of construction paper to one diagonal on the letter X. With a black marking pen, write the letter names of each note on the xylophone.

Y—yarn: Use yellow yarn to embellish a letter Y.

Z—zipper: With zippers closed, glue the fabric portions only of three short zippers to a letter Z. When the glue dries, the zippers will really work!

Eat your words (Activity 84)

Alphabet pancakes and alphabet soup

You will need: (for pancakes) plastic ketchup or mustard container, pancake batter, griddle

(soup) commercially prepared alphabet pasta; homemade vegetable soup

Alphabet pancakes

The next time you serve pancakes, make them extra fun by cooking them in the shape of letters. Spell out your kids' names or a short message by squeezing the batter out in letter shapes using a ketchup or mustard container. You may wish to squeeze the letters out backwards for the best-looking pancakes.

Alphabet soup

Add commercially prepared alphabet pasta to your next pot of homemade soup, and see who can spell the most words!

Alpha-sticks (Activity 85)

Find letters in nature

You will need: found items in the shape of letters from a nature walk

On your next nature walk, scout around for twigs, branches, and driftwood in the shape of letters. The kids will have their eyes glued to the path during the hunt. Bring nature's letters home with you and display them on a shelf, play school with them, and, if you have a large collection, try to spell your name!

Book-worming-it (Activity 86)

Make a reading progress chart

You will need: large sheet of poster board
felt-tipped markers in a variety of colors
stickers (optional)

Challenge your school-age children to read with a reading progress chart. You'll have fun making the chart together, and the children will look forward to filling in each day to reach their goal—and their reward!

Lay the poster board horizontally on your work surface. Have your child draw a long, squiggly bookworm across the top. Then draw a large grid on the rest of the poster board. Print the days of the week along the left side of the grid (see illustration). Decide on some goals and rewards.

Base the reading progress by recording the number of minutes read each day or the number of pages read. Set a goal, and when it is reached, reward the children with something for which they were aiming, such as a new book, an ice cream cone, or going out for pizza.

All children benefit from being read to. You might wish to adapt this activity to recording the number of books you and your child read together. (This involves parents in goal setting and in spending time with kids!) For your preschooler, color in a square or stick on a sticker for each book read. Reward both child and adult by doing something special together!

Surprise in a box (Activity 87)

Lunch box surprises

You will need: family photos, cartoons, paper and pen

When school starts in the fall, make the transition easier for your kids, especially the younger ones, with special lunch box surprises. It's a nice treat to continue throughout the year, too!

Tape a picture of your family to the inside of your child's lunch box. The snapshot may be of some fun activity you shared during the past summer, or it could be a silly photo that is guaranteed to get a laugh from your youngster. This is especially nice to do for children who are going off to school for the first time. A picture of the family can remind them they aren't alone, and they might enjoy showing the family picture to friends and teachers.

Cut out a favorite comic strip or cartoon from the Sunday paper, or write a joke or riddle on a small piece of paper and tuck it in the lunch box between a sandwich and an apple. Or, write short, thoughtful notes such as "Good luck on your spelling test," "I'm looking forward to your birthday party this weekend," or "I love you," and stick them in the lunch box. Your special attention getters are sure to make lunchtime a highlight of the day. (Moms and dads might enjoy some surprises in their lunches too!)

Dial a picture (Activity 88)

Make a picture phone book

You will need: 3″ x 5″ notecards or pieces of plain paper

pictures of children's friends

felt-tipped markers or crayons

paper punch

ribbon or string

Your kids can make their own phone directory even if they aren't quite reading yet. Instead of writing the names in a traditional phone/address book, glue school pictures or draw pictures of friends they might call on notecards. Next to the picture write the child's name and telephone number in large, clear letters. You might add emergency numbers by appropriate pictures. Your kids can keep their special directory next to the phone with the city phone book.

Be sure to discuss phone rules and etiquette with young children. They should understand that the phone is not a toy and should only be used with permission. For older children, you may wish to post rules by the phone, including the maximum length of calls, appropriate times for calling people, and the correct way to answer the phone.

Coupon coup (Activity 89)

"A gift for you" booklet

You will need: 6 pieces of paper, 2" x 5"
2 pieces of construction pa-
per, 2" x 5"
felt-tipped markers
stapler and staples
regular letter size envelope
stickers (optional)

Make a packet of coupons as a special gift for Mom, Dad, or anyone else who is special. This is an ideal gift for birthdays, Christmas, Valentine's Day or Mother's and Father's Day. Add a snappy cover to the packet, and it makes a pretty card too!

Let the kids come up with six ideas for things they can do for the person receiving the gift, like completing some chore around the house, running an errand, babysitting a sibling, or even singing a song or giving a hug. They can also consider giving the gift of time: "This coupon is worth 10 minutes of playing ball with Andrew when Dad comes home" or "This coupon is worth one bike ride around the lake with Annie." Each idea should be written on a piece of paper, and decorations can be added. For fun, they might write "No expiration date" on the bottom.

Staple the coupons together between two pieces of construction paper. Then have the kids write on the cover a message suitable for the occasion (Happy Birthday! Be My Valentine, etc.) and decorate the cover with drawings or stickers or whatever they wish.

Put the coupon book in an envelope and deliver it with a hug!

Sew what? (Activity 90)

Make a card from sewing scraps

You will need: 8½″ x 11″ piece of construction paper

various fabric scraps, ribbon, rick-rack, lace, yarn

buttons, sequins, beads

glitter

shiny or textured paper

glue

scissors

felt-tipped markers or crayons

If a special occasion is coming up, consider making a unique card that reflects the interests of the person and uses up some sewing scraps at the same time!

Cover the work surface with newspaper and set out all the gathered supplies. Think for a few minutes about the person who will receive the card. What are the person's hobbies or interests? Then create from the various scrap material a picture that reflects the person. Glue on fabric shapes, add a ribbon or two, and jazz it all up with a dash of glitter. When satisfied with the masterpiece, set it aside to dry. Once it is dry, add a greeting to the inside and sign it. Place it in an envelope or attach it to the top of a wrapped gift as a clever decoration.

Bubbling over (Activity 91)

Make a bubble card

You will need: pie pan
liquid tempera paint in a variety of colors (blue is good for making clouds and water)
liquid dishwashing detergent
felt-tipped markers or crayons
white or light-colored construction paper
drinking straws
newspaper

Here's a unique and fun way to paint. If your kids like blowing bubbles, they'll love this activity.

Cover your work surface with newspaper. Stir together 1 cup water, 2 tablespoons paint, and 1 tablespoon detergent in the pie pan. Place one end of a straw in the mixture. (Caution the children not to suck on the straw, as they are accustomed to doing when drinking a beverage.) Continue blowing until the bubbles are almost billowing over the edge of the pan. Remove straw and place on newspaper.

Fold a piece of construction paper in half to form a card. Gently place the front of the card on top of the bubbles and hold it in place until several bubbles have popped and transferred their shape onto the paper. Continue the process with different colors, if you wish. Blow more bubbles as needed. If the bubble prints are not as dark as you'd like, add more paint to the mixture. When satisfied with the bubble prints, set aside to dry.

When dry, add drawings to the bubble prints such as a jet flying through the clouds for a "Bon Voyage" card. Write a greeting inside the card and sign it. A unique greeting is ready for delivery!

Pop-up cards

You will need: typing paper
construction paper
scissors
glue
felt-tipped markers or crayons

Kids will enjoy creating a card with a surprise inside. In fact, this card can be more fun than the gift it's attached to.

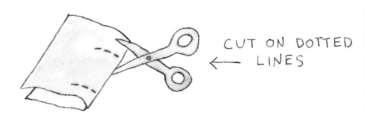

CUT ON DOTTED
← LINES

CENTER SECTION
OF TYPING PAPER
FOLDS OUT AND
IS NOT GLUED DOWN

FOLDED CONSTRUCTION
PAPER
WITH TYPING PAPER
FOLDING OUT

Loosely fold a piece of plain typing paper in half. Starting at the fold, cut two slits about 3" long, 2" from the top and bottom of the folded paper (see illustration). Form a hard crease in the typing paper between the two cuts. Open up the typing paper and glue it down flat to a piece of construction paper, leaving the area between the cuts free. (Be sure the typing paper folds *out*; see illustration.) Fold the construction paper in half so the typing paper is on the inside. (The folded area of the typing paper should still point *out*, not in toward the crease in the construction paper.) Open the card to see if the middle section of the typing paper pops out.

Think of an action such as shooting a basket, hitting a baseball into the stands, or watching a bird fly onto a tree branch. With markers or crayons, draw a picture of your idea on the front of the card. Then draw the picture in action on the inside. For example, place a cut-out of a basketball on the pop-out fold and draw a basket in the top corner of the card. When the card is opened it will appear as if the ball is going toward the hoop. Add a greeting to the card and sign it.

A timely gift (Activity 93)

Time-capsule greeting for a new baby

You will need: large plain envelope
current fashion magazine
current gift or food catalog showing popular products and their prices
front page, sports page, TV guide, and comics section from the paper printed the day the baby was born
snapshots of your family, the neighborhood, the baby's family and home and car
felt-tipped markers or crayons
ribbon and bow

Put together an unusual greeting for a new baby on the block (or a new baby in your home). Years later, it will offer the person a peek into his or her past.

Collect the above items and any other personalized or timely items you can think of (picture of the hospital, postcards from your community, new-issue postage stamps, etc.) and put them in the envelope. Decorate the envelope with pretty designs and add the baby's name. Attach a ribbon and bow and deliver.

Face it (Activity 94)

Cover stains with a child's self-portrait

You will need: stained shirt or new shirt, if you wish (100% cotton works best)
2 or more colors of fabric paint in squeeze bottles
plain drawing paper and pencil
carbon transfer paper (available at fabric and craft stores)
waxed paper or cardboard
ribbon, buttons, hair barrettes, etc. (optional)

CARDBOARD

Are you frustrated by stains that have ruined an otherwise perfect shirt? Incorporate the stain in a portrait of your child!

Have the child draw a self-portrait on the drawing paper. Then place a piece of waxed paper or cardboard between the two layers of the shirt to protect the backside from any paint that might soak through. Using the child's self-portrait as a guide, lightly copy the drawing onto the shirt with a pencil, or trace the drawing on the shirt with carbon paper made for embroidery work (the carbon paper lines will wash out). When drawing on the shirt, try to incorporate the stain (as an eye or nose or under hair, etc.).

Once the drawing is transferred to the shirt, squeeze out paint along the pencil lines. Allow each color to dry before proceeding to the next color. When the entire portrait is dry, embellish it with ribbons in the hair, a bow tie at the neck, or buttons on a shirt, etc. You might want to make a shirt for each member of the family.

Look on the bright side (Activity 95)

Shine copper

You will need: 5 tablespoons salt
½ cup vinegar
1 small mixing bowl
1 slotted spoon
pennies, copper bowls, small copper pitchers, and other small copper objects
newspaper and paper towels

Preschoolers can be introduced to the exciting world of science with this easy and safe chemistry experiment. Your kids will be amazed to see a dingy penny or copper pot transformed magically into a shiny new object, and you may even get a few of your neglected copper pieces polished at the same time!

Cover your work surface with newspaper. Mix together ½ cup vinegar and 5 tablespoons salt in the bowl. Drop some tarnished pennies or small copper objects into the bowl, stirring them around in the mixture. Almost instantly they will change color. Remove the objects with a slotted spoon and place them on a piece of toweling to dry. To shine larger copper objects, dip a soft cloth in the solution and rub it on the item.

Destructo (Activity 96)

Take apart old machines

You will need: small appliance or mechanical object that no longer works (alarm clock, watch, wind-up toy, hand mixer, etc.)
hammer, screwdriver, plier
newspaper

Curiosity encourages creativity. After doing this activity, your kids may be inspired to design their own machines! In any case, if you and your children have always wondered what's under an adding machine or what's behind the face of an alarm clock, give this activity a try.

Place the machine on a work surface covered with newspaper. With screwdrivers, hammers, and pliers, remove the cover of the machine and begin exploring. If the machine has an electrical cord, clip it off for safety's sake. Remove and dispose of any old batteries and glass parts. Try to figure out how the machine works and enjoy speculating on its mysteries. If the machine has small and sharp parts, don't leave it for your preschoolers to explore without adult supervision.

Solar designs (Activity 97)

Make a work of art with the help of the sun

You will need: blueprint paper (available from office supply stores)
"found" nature items (leaves, flowers, sticks, etc.)
"found" household items (keys, nails, screws, paperclips, jewelry, etc.)
clipboard
sunny day

This is *not* a rainy day activity!

While indoors, attach the blueprint paper to a clipboard to hold it in place. Arrange specially collected objects (leaves, flowers, sticks) on the paper. Set the blueprint paper and objects outdoors in direct sunlight for several minutes. Bring them indoors and remove the objects. Prints of the objects now appear on the paper! Make more solar prints using objects from around the house such as keys, nails, screws, jewelry, paperclips, etc.

This project can be done on a less dramatic scale using colored construction paper. Leave the paper in the sun for a few hours for maximum effect.

Bathtub science trick

You will need: bathtub or small wading
pool filled with water
tall paper cup
facial tissue or hankie

Amaze your friends! Impress your relatives! Try this easy but surprising trick at your next party.

Stuff a piece of facial tissue or a hankie into the bottom of a tall paper cup. Turn the cup upside down and submerge it directly into a bathtub or backyard wading pool filled with water. Push the cup all the way to the bottom of the tub or pool and bring it straight up and out of the water. Pull the tissue or hankie out of the cup. It is perfectly dry! (The key to success is to keep the cup perfectly straight when plunging it into the water and pulling it out again.)

PUSH
STRAIGHT
DOWN

← TISSUE

The Amazing JON

Bubbling over (Activity 99)

Make a bubble beard

You will need: wet washcloth
  bar of hand soap

Nothing can top this bathtub activity for laughs and fun!

Rub hand soap generously on one side of a very wet washcloth. Hold the washcloth up to your mouth with the soapy side facing away from you. Blow gently through the washcloth. As you blow, a magnificent bubble beard will begin to grow on the washcloth. If you keep blowing, the beard will drape several inches and become fuller and fuller. Add more water to the washcloth or more soap if necessary. When the kids want to make their own bubble beards, caution them to blow through the washcloth, instead of inhaling.

Clean cream (Activity 100)

Shaving cream bath paint

You will need: muffin tin
spoon
can of shaving cream
food coloring (variety of colors)

For a special bath time treat, mix up some shaving cream bath paints. The kids will love creating silly pictures on the tub and tiles during bath time. And the clean up is simple—just wipe off with water and send paint down the drain!

Squirt shaving cream dollops into each section of a muffin tin. Add a couple of drops of food coloring to each section and mix together with a spoon. Place the tin where kids can reach it while in the bathtub. Let them dip their fingers, hands, or sponges into the paints and create pictures on the walls and tub. When bath time is over, be sure to rinse away the paint.

Index